W9-BME-636

A FIELD GUIDE TO

LONG ISLAND'S FRESHWATER WETLANDS

by

PAMELA G. STEWART
and
LINDA SPRINGER-RUSHIA

Illustrations by Maria T. Weisenberg
Introduction by Glenn A. Richard

Museum of Long Island Natural Sciences
Stony Brook, New York

A Field Guide to Long Island's Freshwater Wetlands

Published by
Museum of Long Island Natural Sciences
State University of New York at Stony Brook
Stony Brook, New York 11794-2100
© 1998 by Museum of Long Island Natural Sciences
All rights reserved. Published 1998
Printed in the United States of America

08 07 06 05 04 03 02 01 00 99 98   5 4 3 2 1

Library of Congress Catalog Card Number: 98-84943

ISBN 1-892170-05-1

STATE UNIVERSITY OF NEW YORK

The State University of New York is an AA/EEO employer.
This publication can be made available in alternative format upon request.

ACKNOWLEDGEMENTS

This sequel to our first publication, *A Field Guide to Long Island's Woodlands,* could not have been completed successfully without the collaborative efforts of the dedicated individuals cited below:

Ann Lattimore of the Mineral Physics Institute, Center for High Pressure Research, for generously providing her desktop publishing talents; **Jeanne Perry**, for contributing her efforts, especially on the Index and compilation of information for the Glossary; **Jean Cole** for donating her Mondays to assist in research and editing; **Alice Balsdon**, for volunteering her time to help with editing; **Douglas V. Winkler**, Director of the Museum of Long Island Natural Sciences, for his knowledgable advice and encouragement on the project. And last, but not least, **Glenn A. Richard**, Educational Coordinator, Mineral Physics Institute, Center for High Pressure Research, whose text on Ferns and Introduction, complete with his graphics, are invaluable additions to *A Field Guide to Long Island's Freshwater Wetlands."* Glenn's counsel, expertise and unflagging committment were an inspiration.

Thank you, each and everyone.

TABLE OF CONTENTS

INTRODUCTION

Where Land and Water Meet

Wetlands are a meeting place between land and water, the two most contrasting types of material that cover the Earth's surface. Wetlands are, in fact, a hybrid of both, and because land and water differ so markedly both physically and chemically, the resulting combination forms a very interesting and diverse array of environments.

While the aesthetic value of wetlands is a subjective matter, many people appreciate them for their beauty. They offer us dark silhouettes of trees and cattails during colorful sunsets, the chorus of spring peepers as the world reawakens in March and April, the aroma of Sweet Pepperbush, the graceful beauty of herons and egrets, the tart taste of cranberries in autumn, the flaming red of maple and tupelo in October, cold stark icy winter landscapes. The importance of the contribution that the enjoyment of wetlands makes to the quality of our lives is immeasurable.

What is Covered by this Book

The study of wetlands is a vast topic, and no book can present a comprehensive treatment of them. Wetlands occur under a wide variety of conditions: climate, substrate, water chemistry, wave activity, flow rate of water, tidal regime, and biological context. Wetlands exist in the tropics, the arctic, and at numerous localities in between. In altitude, they range from sea level to thousands of feet in elevation. The water they contain may be fresh, or may be characterized by a salt content higher than that of the oceans. Many wetlands along the coast, even freshwater ones, are affected by the tides. As a result of this diversity of conditions, they exhibit tremendous variety in their physical and biological makeup.

This book is intended as an introduction to the freshwater wetlands of Long Island. Although salt marshes are an important component of our local natural environment, they are not included here. Even this narrowed scope is aimed at a subject that could form the basis of a lifetime of study and original research. We hope this book will

1

nurture your interest sufficiently to encourage you to learn more by visiting wetlands in your area, and by reading additional books and scientific articles about this fascinating subject.

How to Use this Book

In this book, as in its companion book, *A Field Guide to Long Island's Woodlands,* species of plants that inhabit wetlands are grouped by growth habit or other morphological distinctions. Shrubs and wildflowers are grouped together, while many of the other forms of plants, such as grasses and ferns have their own sections. Animals are grouped taxonomically, with sections devoted to each of the major vertebrate classes, and an additional section for the invertebrates. Common and scientific names are provided for each species, along with pertinent characteristics. Habitats where they occur on Long Island are specified in order to assist you in finding them in their natural settings. Illustrations of each species are provided for your enjoyment and to assist you in their identification. This book is not intended as a complete monograph of our wetlands, but instead presents a sampling of what you are likely to encounter in this type of habitat on Long Island.

What is a Wetland?

Definitions of wetlands abound, due to the wide variety of conditions found among them. This is further complicated by the fact that gradual transitions exist between wetlands and adjacent habitats, such as terrestrial, marine, and lacustrine ecosystems. In general, however, the following attributes can be used to distinguish them from other environments:

In wetlands, water exists either at the surface or within the root zone of plants. The soil or substrate in wetlands is strongly influenced by the presence of water, making it different from that of surrounding habitats.

The plants and animals that inhabit wetlands are adapted to the abundance of water there. Consequently, the presence of certain species can be considered as an indicator of wetland conditions.

Types of Wetlands

Although all wetlands have in common a copious supply of water, they differ markedly in other ways and form a remarkably diverse set of habitats. They can form along bodies of water such as streams or ponds, or they may appear as a wet area surrounded by woodland. Some freshwater wetlands fed by groundwater seepage exist as narrow fringes sandwiched between wooded areas and salt marshes.

The great diversity and complexity of wetlands is reflected in a variety of classification schemes. Most of them are based upon a combination of the type of vegetation present, the chemistry of the water, and the nature of the bottom sediment. Ecologists usually divide wetlands into five broad categories, namely marine, estuarine, riverine, lacustrine, and palustrine. Marine and estuarine wetlands are associated with salt water. In this book, we deal with the other three categories, which represent freshwater wetlands (diagrams, pages 4 and 5).

Lacustrine wetlands refer to standing bodies of water such as lakes and ponds. In a lake or pond, directional flow of water is minimal. In a pond, sufficient sunlight penetrates the water for rooted plants to grow anywhere along the bottom. Accordingly, ponds are rather shallow, and generally do not cover a very large area. Water temperature varies very little with depth in a pond because even a slow rate of movement brings about effective mixing. In contrast, lakes are generally larger than ponds, and include some areas where the water is too deep to allow sufficient sunlight to reach the bottom for plant growth. In addition, during the growing season, the water at the bottom of a lake is usually quite a bit cooler than the water near the surface. This temperature stratification is maintained by the higher density of the cooler water and the lack of heating by sunlight near the bottom (diagram, page 6).

The fauna and flora on the shallow edges of small lakes are often similar to that of ponds. The edges of ponds and lakes also may support marshes and swamps. Lacustrine wetlands often are fed by and empty into rivers and streams.

Types of Wetlands

Pond: Shallow enough for rooted vegetation to grow throughout the bottom

Rooted vegetation

Lake: Too deep for rooted vegetation to grow throughout the bottom

Rooted vegetation

No rooted vegetation

Rooted vegetation

Bog: Mat of acidic peat and live plants floating on a body of water

Bog mat

Bog mat

Central pond

Stream: water flowing in a channel

Stream channel

Types of Wetlands

Pond: Shallow enough for rooted vegetation to grow throughout the bottom

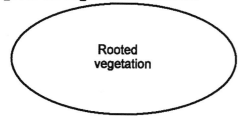

Rooted vegetation

Lake: Too deep for rooted vegetation to grow throughout the bottom

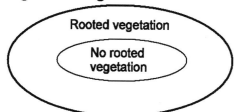

Rooted vegetation

No rooted vegetation

Bog: Mat of acidic peat and live plants floating on a body of water

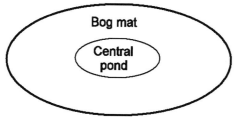

Bog mat

Central pond

Stream: water flowing in a channel

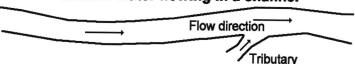

Flow direction

Tributary

Zonation of Vegetation in a Lake

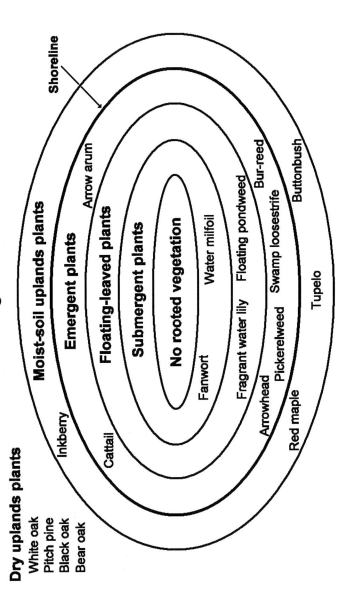

Dry uplands plants
White oak
Pitch pine
Black oak
Bear oak

Moist-soil uplands plants
Inkberry

Emergent plants
Cattail
Arrow arum

Floating-leaved plants
Fanwort

Submergent plants
Fragrant water lily
Water milfoil
Floating pondweed

No rooted vegetation

Arrowhead
Pickerelweed
Swamp loosestrife
Bur-reed

Red maple
Tupelo
Buttonbush

Shoreline

6

Zonation of Vegetation in a Pond

Emergent plants

Floating-leaved plants

Submergent plants

Cattail

Arrowhead

Floating pondweed

Fragrant water lily

Fanwort   Water milfoil

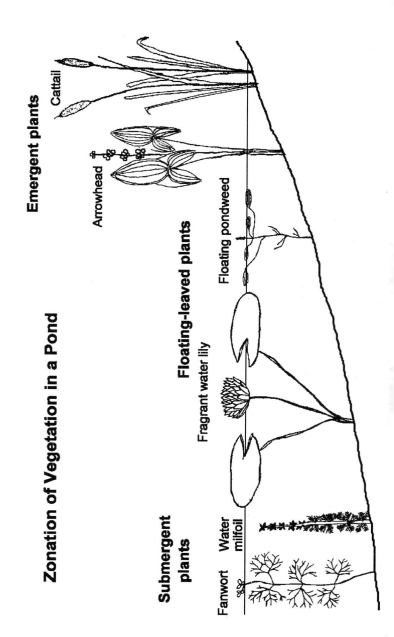

7

Vegetation of ponds and the edges of lakes often occurs in distinct zones according to growth habit. In the deepest zone is submergent vegetation, such as Water Milfoil and Fanwort. These plants are nearly completely covered by water. With Fanwort, only the flowers break the surface. Closer to the shore is the floating-leaf plant zone. Here, plants are rooted in the bottom, but at least some of their leaves float on the water's surface. Examples include Floating-leaved Pondweed and Fragrant Water Lily. Insects, snails, flatworms, hydras, and other fauna often live on or under the floating leaves. Immediately adjacent to the shoreline is the zone of emergent plants. The vegetation is rooted in the substrate beneath the water, but the stems and leaves of the plants project above the water surface. Fish, frogs, insects, crayfish, and other animals live among the underwater parts of these plants. Birds and dragonflies alight on the exposed stems. On Long Island, examples of emergent plants abound, and include cattails, Pickerelweed, Arrowhead, Arrow-arum, and Swamp Loosestrife (diagram, page 7).

Riverine wetlands are associated with rivers and streams. These bodies of water are narrow compared to their length, and nearly always exhibit a significant directional flow of water, which is controlled by gravity. Accordingly, the steepness of the terrain has a strong influence on the rate of flow. On Long Island, slopes are usually gradual, and therefore currents are not very swift along most stretches of our riverine wetlands. However, on the hilly moraines, or where dams create spillways, currents may be rapid. In these fast moving sections, submerged plants are often characterized by strap-like leaves that can withstand currents without being torn. While the rate of flow may vary over time, in most freshwater streams the direction of flow remains constant. Exceptions are freshwater tidal streams such as the Nissequogue River, where the nearly twice-daily rise and fall of water in Long Island Sound brings about tidal fluctuations at the mouth of the river, and even in a large portion of the freshwater section. The velocity and quantity of flow varies seasonally in Long Island's streams and rivers. During early spring the Peconic River typically experiences a flow rate equal to double the amount that usually occurs in early autumn.

Palustrine wetlands are quite diverse, and include swamps, marshes and bogs. Water in these wetlands is shallow or beneath the substrate, and flow is minimal. Sediment may be highly organic, or may consist of varying amounts of clay, silt, and sand.

Swamps are characterized by a dense growth of trees, which may be growing in wet soil, peat or standing water. The water may range from very acid to nearly neutral in pH. On Long Island, maple-tupelo swamps are common, while Atlantic White Cedar swamps are rare. Even more unusual is the pine swamp at Mashomack Preserve on Shelter Island, where White Pine (*Pinus strobus*), which is rare in the natural setting on Long Island and almost always grows in uplands, is found growing in a wetland.

Marshes are dominated by grasses, sedges, or rushes as well as an abundance of other herbaceous, or soft-tissued, plant species. They may also contain shrubs, but trees are not present in large numbers. On Long Island, typical plant species include cattails, sedges, rushes, Steeplebush, and others that also occur in the emergent plant zone of ponds and lakes. Marshes may be classified further into rich fens, which contain an abundance of plant nutrients, or poor fens where nutrients are scarcer.

Bogs are highly acidic wetlands where peat is accumulating due to the very slow decay of plant material. The peat is covered by a layer of live sphagnum mosses. Growing within this mat of moss and peat are sedges, rushes, an unusual variety of other herbaceous plants, and shrubs. Decay is inhibited by the acidity of the water and its low levels of dissolved oxygen. Nutrients are chemically locked up in the peat, making them largely unavailable to plants. Therefore, some species exhibit unusual adaptations for obtaining essential elements. Sundews, bladderworts, and Pitcher Plants have mechanisms for capturing tiny animals and digesting them in order to supplement their diets with nutrients such as nitrates. Legumes and Sweet Gale (*Myrica gale*) harbor nitrogen-fixing bacteria on their roots. In a bog, the entire mat of peat, sphagnum and rooted plants floats on top of an underlying body of water, and if a person jumps up and down on it, the mat ripples like a waterbed (diagram, page 10).

Relationship of Wetlands to Groundwater on Long Island

On Long Island, most wetlands are surface expressions of the water table.

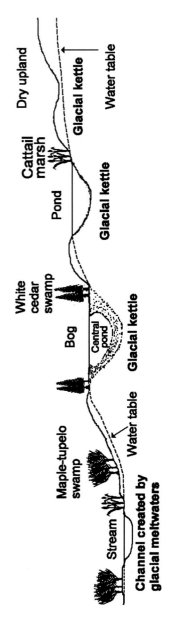

Upper Glacial Aquifer

10

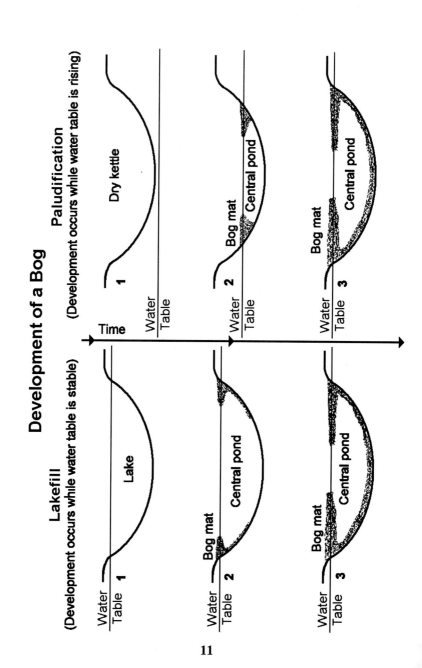

Development of a Bog

Lakefill
(Development occurs while water table is stable)

Paludification
(Development occurs while water table is rising)

Time

1 Lake — Water Table

1 Dry kettle — Water Table

2 Bog mat — Central pond — Water Table

2 Bog mat — Central pond — Water Table

3 Bog mat — Central pond — Water Table

3 Bog mat — Central pond — Water Table

11

The Geologic Context

The origin of wetlands is largely controlled by the local geology. Beneath the surface of Long Island lie trillions of gallons of water which fill the pore spaces between grains of sand and gravel that make up the Island. The upper surface of this reservoir of water is known as the water table. In places where the land surface lies at a low elevation, the water table is exposed. It is here that wetlands form (diagram, page 11).

Nearly all of Long Island's surface was formed by giant sheets of ice, known as continental glaciers, which began to melt away about 21,000 years ago. While the last continental glacier was at its maximum extent, its southern edge was on Long Island. Along the North Shore and through the center of the Island are moraines, where material pushed by the glacier forms a hilly terrain. Other areas called outwash plains are flatter, where meltwater that issued from the glacier deposited sand and gravel in coalescing deltas. Wetlands may develop where glacial meltwaters formed valleys that now intersect the water table, harboring streams. Where blocks of ice from the glacier became buried, and subsequently melted, depressions known as kettles formed. Ponds and lakes exist where kettles now penetrate the water table. Wetlands also exist in other low areas within the Long Island Pine Barrens. The geological origins of these shallow depressions is currently a subject of debate among geologists.

Wetlands also existed in Long Island's geologic past. During the Cretaceous period, over 60 million years ago, when dinosaurs were at their greatest diversity and abundance, the area that is now Long Island was the site of a vast delta, where a river or a series of streams that drained eastern North America deposited fine sediments. Recently, a dinosaur fossil was found on Long Island, and the species it represents may very well have lived in these wetlands.

Places of Refuge

The Calverton Ponds in Long Island's Central Pine Barrens region serve as a refuge for the highest concentration of rare, threatened and endangered species of plants and animals in New York State. They are prime examples of coastal plain ponds, an unusual type of wetland that occurs in several localities along the East Coast of the United States. These ponds are shallow and do not exhibit the typical upside-down helmet-shaped profile of kettle ponds. Therefore, it seems unlikely that they were formed by stranded, partially buried blocks of ice.

During times of drought, the water level drops in these ponds, and areas near their edges, usually covered by water, become exposed. It is during these episodes of low water that many of the rare species of plants appear on these exposed pondshores. Sundews (*Drosera* spp.), Virginia Meadow Beauty (*Rhexia virginica*), and bladderworts (*Utricularia* spp.) suddenly appear in great abundance. If the drought persists, however, woody plants such as Red Maple (*Acer rubrum*) begin to colonize these exposed areas, and the rare species become shaded and crowded out. Ultimately, within a few years, precipitation increases to normal levels, and the pondshore becomes submerged once again. This drowns both the woody plants and the rare species. However, in doing so, it clears the pondshore, leaving it ready for the rare species to flourish during the next drought.

The Importance of Wetlands

Wetlands have tremendous ecological, recreational, and economic value. However, the importance of wetlands has not always been recognized. Over half of the wetlands that originally existed in the United States have been destroyed since Europeans colonized North America. Fortunately, today a great deal of legislation exists that is designed to protect wetlands. On Long Island, our wetlands are protected by the New York State Freshwater Wetlands Act, and by the New York State Tidal Wetlands Act.

Many wetlands are sites of high biological productivity. Aided by sunlight, green plants photosynthesize to convert nutrients into living material. As the basis of the food web, this plant material may be eaten by animals. Freshwater tidal marshes are among the most productive wetlands in the world.

In addition, wetlands are important reservoirs of biodiversity. Bogs are habitats for unusual species of plants that are adapted to the special physical and chemical conditions that exist there. And, as already stated, coastal plain ponds on Long Island are the home of some of the rarest plants and animals in New York State.

Wetlands are also breeding areas for many species of animals including mammals, birds, turtles, frogs, salamanders, fish, and insects. Since each type of wetland favors the breeding of particular species, it is important to preserve a diversity of wetland types.

Many of the plants in wetlands absorb pollutants from the environment. Both fresh and salt water tidal marshes remove contaminants from terrestrial runoff as it approaches the shoreline. This helps to protect Long Island Sound and our bays from high levels of nitrates and other materials.

Visiting a Wetland

With proper preparation and a few precautions, a visit to a wetland can be a fascinating experience. It is important to remember that you are likely to become wet and muddy during your explorations - dress appropriately. Be aware that Poison Sumac and Poison Ivy are present in some Long Island wetlands, and that mosquitos may be present seasonally. Field guides, binoculars, and a hand lens can enhance your experience. You also might want to record your observations with a camera, a notebook, or a small tape recorder.

Remember that when you visit any natural environment, you should respect its integrity and strive to create as little impact as possible, staying on paths or boardwalks. Do not remove or disturb plants, animals or rocks, and be sure not to leave any litter. You should also refrain from feeding animals.

Plant Species

TREES - Tall, woody plants with single or divided trunk and numerous branches, minimum adult height 15-20 feet; deciduous or evergreen.

Atlantic White Cedar (*Chamaecyparis thyoides*)
Evergreen   Height: up to 80 ft.   Monoecious
Coniferous; tapering, with fibrous, ridged, reddish-brown bark and scaly blue-green foliage covering branches. Cones very small, ball-shaped, bluish, turning dark red-brown. Once abundant on Long Island.
Habitat: Swamps

Red Maple (*Acer rubrum*)
Deciduous   Height: up to 90 ft.   Monoecious
Shade tree; frequently multiple-trunked; smooth gray bark, cracked, scaly ridges with age, reddish twigs. Leaves opposite, green, rounded, 3 prominent lobes, 2 smaller lobes at leaf bottom, deep red in autumn. Red flowers in clusters before leaves open, early spring. Winged fruit in pairs, 1", May-July.
Habitat: Swamps, shorelines

Sweetgum (*Liquidambar styraciflua*)
Deciduous   Height: up to 130 ft.   Monoecious
Grayish or brown furrowed bark; branches often corky-winged; sap sweet, hardening to chewable gum. Leaves alternate, 5"-7", starlike, with 5-7 pointed lobes, serrate, fragrant when crushed. Flowers tiny, green, globular clusters. Fruit dry, prickly, spiny long-stemmed, hanging ball.
Habitat: Shorelines, swamps

Tupelo, Sour Gum or Black Gum (*Nyssa sylvatica*)
Deciduous   Height: up to 100 ft.   Monoecious
Flat-topped, with twisted, horizontal branches; dark, deeply-grooved, ridged bark. Leaves 2"-5", alternate, oval, shiny, toothless, bright red late summer to fall. Flowers green, inconspicuous. Fruit dark blue drupes on end of branch.
Habitat: Swamps, shorelines

Weeping Willow (*Salix babylonica*)
Deciduous   Height: up to 70 ft.   Dioecious
Introduced from China via Europe, naturalized in many areas; distinguished by rounded crown of slender, long, drooping branches. Bark grayish-brown, heavily ridged. Leaves alternate, narrow, 1"-5", long-pointed lanceolate, hairless, light green, whitish beneath. Flowers greenish catkins. Fruit tiny hairy seeds.
Habitat: Shorelines

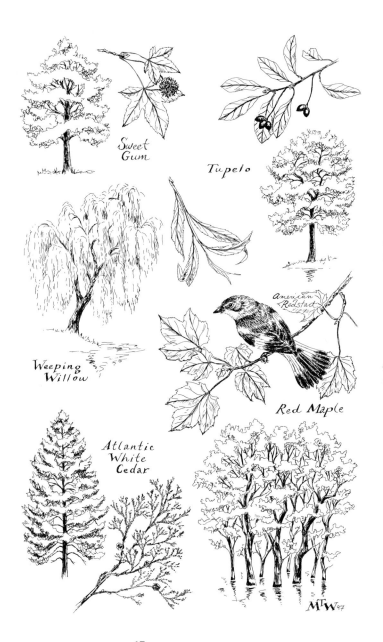

Sweet
Gum

Tupelo

Weeping
Willow

American
Redstart

Red Maple

Atlantic
White
Cedar

M^TW97

17

SHRUBS - Woody plants, less than 15-20 ft. in height, normally with several trunks and numerous branches.

WILDFLOWERS - Blooming herbaceous plants, sometimes annual but most often perennial.

Arrow-arum (*Peltandra virginica*)
Wildflower   Height: up to 2 ft.   Flowers: Late spring to early summer
Common stemless emergent found along shorelines. Leaves large, thick, arrow-shaped, feather-veined. Flowers on slender spadix enveloped by erect, green, wavy-edged spathe. Leaves and flowers on separate stalks arise from thick rootstock. Fruit greenish berry cluster in fall.
Habitat: All wetlands

Broad-leaved Arrowhead (*Sagittaria latifolia*)
Wildflower   Height: up to 4 ft.   Flowers: Mid summer to early fall
Emergent aquatic plant. Leaves above water arrow-shaped with parallel veins; submerged leaves ribbonlike. Flowers on separate stalk, white, 3 petals and sepals, in whorls of 3. Fruit distinctive 3-clustered achene.
Habitat: Marshes, bogs, lakes, ponds, streams

Swamp Azalea (*Rhododendron viscosum*)
Shrub   Height: up to 17 ft.   Flowers: Mid to late summer
Multi-branched tall shrub also called Swamp Honeysuckle. Leaves 1"-4", slightly hairy, shiny, oblong, green, lighter below. Attractive vaselike flowers in terminal clusters, usually white, with protruding stamens, very fragrant. Fruit small dried seed capsule.
Habitat: Swamps, shorelines

Swamp Beggar-tick (*Bidens connata*)
Wildflower   Height: up to 7 ft.   Flowers: Late summer to early fall
Tall branching annual, smooth reddish stem. Leaves opposite, long-stalked, thin, 2"-5", shiny, lanceolate, serrate. Flowers composite orange disc, usually rayless (occasionally 1-5), long outer bracts. Fruit hairy, oblong achene with 2-4 downwardly barbed awns which commonly stick to passersby.
Habitat: Swamps

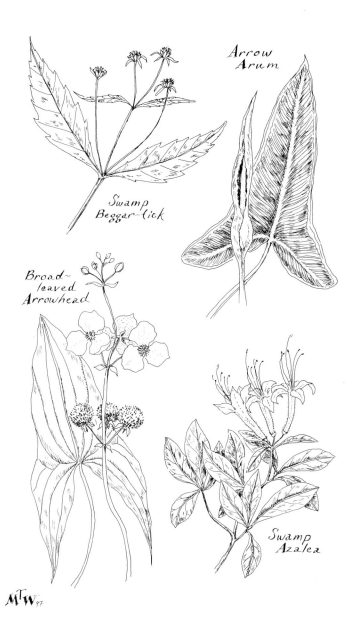

Arrow
Arum

Swamp
Beggar-tick

Broad-
leaved
Arrowhead

Swamp
Azalea

MTW ₉₇

Common Bladderwort (*Utricularia vulgaris*)
Wildflower   Height: up to 6 in   Flowers: Early to mid summer
Submerged, floating, aquatic plant. Fibrous branches with threadlike leaves, bearing hundreds of utricles. Flowers yellow, resemble snapdragon, on single stalk above water. Carnivorous plant; sucks minute animals into utricles equipped with sensitive cilia around entry and rapidly digests prey with enzymes. Nutrients absorbed into stem, resetting "trap".
Habitat: Lakes, ponds

Highbush Blueberry (*Vaccinium corymbosum*)
Shrub   Height: up to 12 ft.   Flowers: Late spring
Locally abundant, often forming dense thickets. Warty twigs; leaves elliptical, pointed, smooth above, slightly hairy underneath. Flowers small, white, bell-shaped, in terminal clusters. Fruit blue to blue-black berries in summer; edible, sweet. Ancestor of many cultivated varieties.
Habitat: Swamps, bogs, shorelines

Blue Flag (*Iris versicolor*)
Wildflower   Height: up to 3 ft. Flowers: Late spring to summer
Common native iris. Leaves, growing from thick rhizome, long, thin, bladelike, grayish-green. Eye-catching violet-blue flowers on erect stem, 3 downward curving sepals often streaked with yellow, 3 narrow upright petals. Fruit 3-lobed capsule.
Habitat: Swamps, marshes, shorelines

Bur-reed (*Sparganium americanum*)
Wildflower   Height: up to 6 ft.   Flowers: All summer
Emergent plant, frequently in thick stands. Leaves long, grasslike, spongy, either erect or floating. Flowers on branching stems, with staminate heads above larger female flowers. Fruit green prickly ball of nutlets.
Habitat: Lakes, ponds, shorelines

Buttonbush (*Cephalanthus occidentalis*)
Shrub   Height: up to 10 ft.   Flowers: Mid to late summer
Easily recognized by its spherical flower head. Leaves oval, pointed, dark green, leathery, opposite or in whorls of 3 or 4; leafstalk reddish. Fragrant flowers white, tiny, clustered in 1" ball-like head. Fruit dry, brown sphere of nutlets in fall, often remaining through winter.
Habitat: Shorelines, swamps

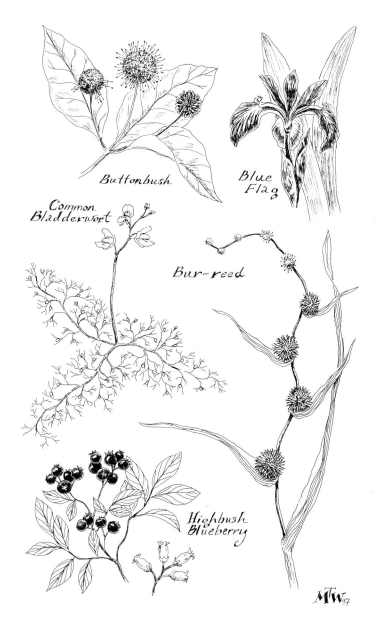

Buttonbush

Blue Flag

Common Bladderwort

Bur-reed

Highbush Blueberry

MTW 97

21

Cardinal-flower (*Lobelia cardinalis*)
Wildflower   Height: up to 5 ft.   Flowers: Mid to late summer
Only bright scarlet flower in Long Island's wetlands; found in small, patchy colonies. Leaves large, alternate, lance-shaped, serrate. Tubular red flowers, upper lip with 2 lobes, lower lip with 3, in elongated clusters on tall spike; primarily pollinated by hummingbirds. Fruit dry pod with many small seeds.
Habitat: Shorelines, marshes, swamps

Broad-leaved Cattail or Common Cattail (*Typha latifolia*)
Wildflower   Height: up to 8 ft.   Flowers: Late spring to mid summer
Tall colonial marsh plant spread by creeping rhizomes. Leaves up to 1" wide, 6' long, flat, erect, lanceolate, sheathing stem in fanlike appearance at base. Flowers monoecious; uppermost yellowish spike of small staminate flowers abut very conspicuous, cigarlike, fuzzy, brown, pistillate head packed with minute flowers. Fruit many tiny seeds with hairs released in fluffy masses.
Habitat: Marshes, ponds

Narrow-leaved Cattail (*Typha angustifolia*)
Wildflower   Height: up to 6 ft.   Flowers: Late spring to mid summer
Similar to Broad-leaved species with noticeable differences. Leaves 6' long but only ½" wide, sheathing stem in cylindrical appearance at base.   Smaller fruiting heads than *T. latifolia,* with gap between staminate and pistillate flowers.   Favors deeper water and more tolerant to pollution.
Habitat: Marshes, ponds

Red Chokeberry (*Aronia arbutifolia*)
Shrub   Height: up to 12 ft.   Flowers: Spring
Thicket-forming shrub with dark, thin, brown stems and gray twigs. Leaves elliptic, serrate, smooth above, wooly beneath with row of tiny glands along midrib. Flowers small, white, in terminal clusters. Fruit small, fleshy red pome remaining on plant into winter.
Habitat: Swamps, bogs

Cranberry (*Vaccinium macrocarpon*)
Shrub   Height: up to 8 in. Flowers: Early to mid summer
Low, creeping, vinelike evergreen. Leaves on erect branches, alternate, small, oval, shiny dark green, leathery. Flowers pinkish-white, nodding, with rolled-back petals, stamens united into long cone. Fruit yellow-green, ripening to dark red edible berry in fall. Once grown commercially on Long Island.
Habitat: Bogs, shorelines

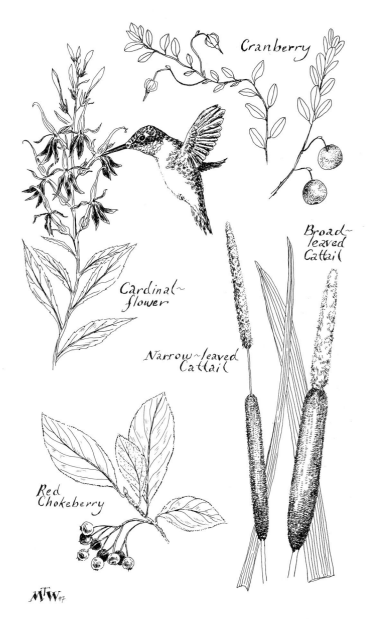

Cranberry

Cardinal~
flower

Broad~
leaved
Cattail

Narrow~leaved
Cattail

Red
Chokeberry

MTW 97

Silky Dogwood (*Cornus amomum*)
Shrub   Height: up to 10 ft.   Flowers: Late spring to early summer
Distinctive wetland plant, purplish twigs and branchlets with silky hairs. Leaves opposite, 1"-5", broadly oval, smooth edged, petioled, strongly veined. Flowers white, small, flat-topped cyme. Fruit round, light blue.
Habitat: Swamps

Common Duckweed (*Lemna* spp.)
Wildflower   Diameter: 1/8 in.   Flowers: Summer
Tiny, floating, aquatic plant, often forming large mats on water's surface. Thallus oval, green, 1 or more dangling rootlets. Flower white, inconspicuous, infrequent to rare. Fruit tiny. Reproduction by division of plant body. Favorite waterfowl food.
Habitat: Marshes, ponds

Common Elderberry (*Sambucus canadensis*)
Shrub   Height: up to 10 ft.   Flowers: Early summer
Identified by warts on bark called lenticels; new twig growth soft, nonwoody. Leaves compound, opposite, 5-11 elliptic, coarse-toothed leaflets. Flowers white, small, fragrant, in flat-topped clusters. Fruit edible, purple-black drupe on red stems in fall.
Habitat: Marshes, swamps, shorelines

Fanwort (*Cabomba caroliniana*)
Wildflower   Flowers: Late spring to late summer
Aquatic submergent plant. Thin branching stem coated with gelatinous matter. Floating leaves narrow, oblong, ½"-¾", alternate or opposite. Submerged leaves broad, shield-shaped, repeatedly divided, 1"-2", whorled or opposite. Flowers white or yellowish, petals ovate, emerge above water on long peduncle.
Habitat: Ponds, lakes, streams

Yellow-eyed Grass (*Xyris torta*)
Wildflower   Height: up to 3 ft.   Flowers: Mid to late summer
Grasslike, with bulbous swelling at plant base. Leaves slender, flat, erect, becoming twisted when mature. Flowers small, yellow, 3 rounded petals, enclosed by leathery scale-like bracts on cone-shaped flower head atop leafless stalk.
Habitat: Bogs, swamps, marshes, shorelines

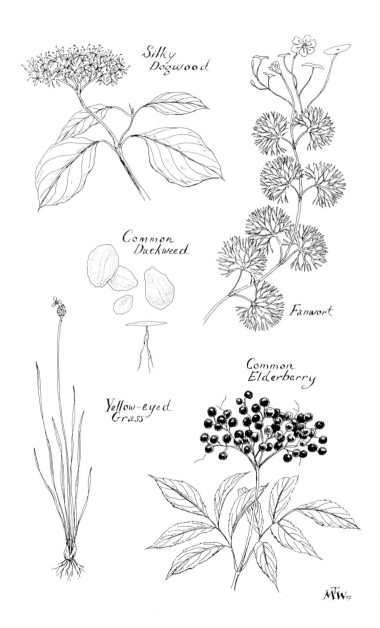

Silky Dogwood

Common Duckweed

Fanwort

Yellow-eyed Grass

Common Elderberry

MTW '97

Golden Hedge-hyssop (*Gratiola aurea*)
Wildflower   Height: up to 15 in.   Flowers: All summer
Low, creeping, semiaquatic herb. Leaves paired, opposite, smooth margins, lancelike, somewhat clasping to stem. Flowers small, bright yellow, trumpet-shaped, solitary, on long stalk from leaf axil. Fruit segmented capsule with numerous seeds.
Habitat: Swamps, shorelines

Inkberry (*Ilex glabra*)
Shrub   Height: up to 10 ft.   Flowers: Late spring to early summer
Dioecious evergreen, type of holly, with gray, finely haired twigs. Leaves 1"-2", alternate, dark green, shiny, leathery, elliptic, notched near tip. Flowers small, greenish-white, innocuous, solitary, on stem from leaf axils. Fruit black drupe; easily stains clothes.
Habitat: Marshes, swamps

Jewelweed or Spotted Touch-me-not (*Impatiens capensis*)
Wildflower   Height: up to 5 ft.   Flowers: All summer
Fragile, bushy, succulent-stemmed annual. Leaves alternate, pale, thin, oval, serrate. Flowers trumpet-shaped, orange with reddish spots, hanging singly on stalk from leaf axils. Fruit capsule; explodes at slightest touch, dispersing numerous seeds up to 8'.
Habitat: Swamps, marshes, shorelines

Spotted Joe-Pye-weed (*Eupatorium maculatum*)
Wildflower Height: up to 6 ft. Flowers: Late summer to early fall
Sturdy, erect, branching perennial with purple spotted stem. Thick leaves long, lanceolate, serrate, in whorls of 3-5. Flowers composite, pinkish-purple, in large, terminal, flat-topped, fuzzy mass. Fruit feathery achene.
Habitat: Swamps, marshes, shorelines

Sheep Laurel (*Kalmia angustifolia*)
Shrub   Height: up to 3 ft.   Flowers: Late spring to early summer
Evergreen with nearly erect branches. Leaves leathery, elliptic, narrow, often drooping, in whorls of 3. Flowers deep pink, cuplike, in clusters along sides of twigs under newer, upright leaves. Fruit 5 lobed dark capsule. Entire plant poisonous if eaten.
Habitat: Swamps, bogs, marshes, shorelines

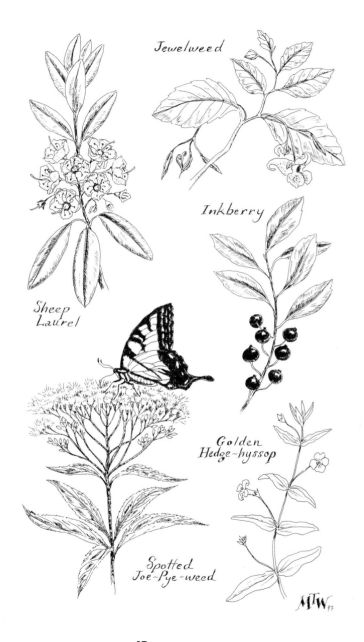

Jewelweed

Inkberry

Sheep
Laurel

Golden
Hedge~hyssop

Spotted
Joe~Pye~weed

MTW 97

Leatherleaf (*Chamaedaphne calyculata*)
Shrub   Height: up to 4 ft.   Flowers: Early to late spring
Low, multi-branched, evergreen with erect, hairless twigs. Leaves thick, narrow, elliptic, yellowish underneath, on main vertical branch. Smaller leaves found on flowering, horizontal branches. Flowers white, bell-shaped, dangling in a row. Fruit small, round capsule.
Habitat: Bogs, swamps

Turk's-cap Lily (*Lilium superbum*)
Wildflower   Height: up to 7 ft.   Flowers: Mid to late summer
Largest native lily; erect flowering stem. Leaves lanceolate, long, smooth. Flowers orange, spotted reddish-brown, long stamens, dangling brown anthers, petals and sepals recurved. Green star in center of flower. Fruit podlike capsules.
Habitat: Marshes

Swamp Loosestrife (*Decodon verticillatus*)
Shrub   Height: up to 10 ft.   Flowers: Mid to late summer
Thicket-forming, semiaquatic; ridged, arching branches root at tip when they touch water or mud. Leaves 2"-5", lanceolate, in pairs or 3's, slightly hairy underneath. Flowers lavender, bell-shaped, tufted in upper leaf axils. Fruit round capsule in fall.
Habitat: Shorelines, swamps

Marsh Marigold or Cowslip (*Caltha palustris*)
Wildflower   Height: up to 2 ft.   Flowers: Spring
Herald of spring, often in large stands. Leaves shiny, broad, roundish or heart-shaped on hollow, succulent, branched stems. Flowers brilliant "Buttercup" yellow, waxy, shallow cup-shaped, 5-10 petal-like sepals that close at night. Fruit in whorl. Thrives in waterlogged soil. Toxic to animals.
Habitat: Shorelines, swamps, marshes

Virginia Meadow-beauty (*Rhexia virginica*)
Wildflower   Height: up to 2 ft.   Flowers: Mid to late summer
Low, sturdy; hairy, 4-sided, winged stem. Leaves opposite, ovate, serrate, prominently veined. Flowers deep rose to purple, in terminal clusters, 4 petals, 8 yellow protruding stamens. Fruit vase-shaped capsule.
Habitat: Shorelines, swamps

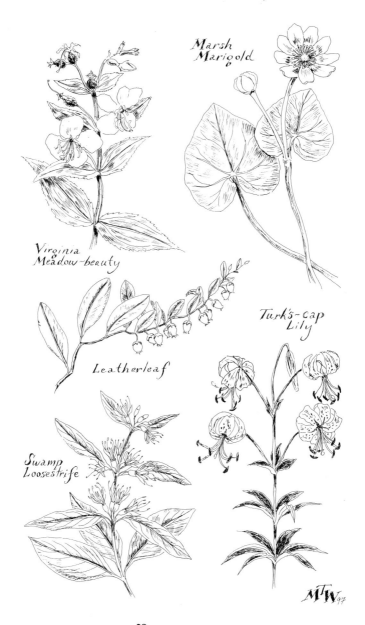

Marsh
Marigold

Virginia
Meadow~beauty

Leatherleaf

Turk's-cap
Lily

Swamp
Loosestrife

MTW 97

29

Swamp Milkweed (*Asclepias incarnata*)
Wildflower   Height: up to 4 ft.   Flowers: All summer
Only wetlands milkweed; stem milk sparse. Leaves opposite, smooth, lanceolate, narrow, on branched, sometimes hairy stem. Flowers dark pink in small umbrella-like terminal clusters, 5 recurved petals and raised crown. Fruit long, tapering pod holding numerous seeds attached to silky hairs.
Habitat: Swamps, marshes, shorelines

Orchid
Wildflower   Height: variable   Flowers: Early to mid summer
Usually tropical, stemless perennial, typically with basal leaves and showy flowers; on L.I. relies on root fungus symbiosis.
Habitat: Bogs, swamps

Arethusa or Dragon's Mouth (*Arethusa bulbosa*)
Small, uncommon, up to 12" high, develops from small bulb. Leaf single, grasslike, appearing after flower. Bloom magenta-pink, 2", solitary, 3 erect sepals and hood over drooping yellowish, fringed, purple-blotched lip. Fruit 6-ribbed elliptic capsule.

Grass Pink (*Calopogon pulchellus*)
Common, up to 20" high, from round bulb. Leaf single, lanceolate, sheathing flower stalk. Multiple 1" blooms in a raceme, purplish-pink, fragrant, sepals and petals similar, erect yellow bearded lip uppermost. Fruit oblong capsule.

Rose Pogonia or Snake-mouth (*Pogonia ophioglossoides*)
Common, up to 20" high, from rhizomes. Usually with single, erect, lance-shaped leaf midway up stalk. Flowers less than 1", solitary or paired, slightly nodding, pale pink, lip yellow, pink fringed, below petals and sepals. Fruit ovoid capsule. Often grows with Grass Pink.

Pickerelweed (*Pontederia cordata*)
Wildflower   Height: up to 4 ft.   Flowers: All summer
Aquatic emergent with hollow stems for buoyancy. Single leaf glossy, heart-shaped, veined, up to 10". Flowers bluish-violet, numerous, tubular, borne on terminal 3"-4" spadix. Blooms open progressively from bottom up. Fruit one-seeded utricle in flower base.
Habitat: Marshes, shorelines

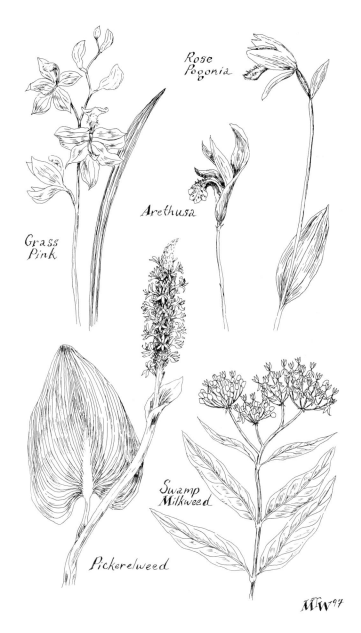

Rose
Pogonia

Grass
Pink

Arethusa

Swamp
Milkweed

Pickerelweed

MW 97

Sweet Pepperbush (*Clethra alnifolia*)
Shrub   Height: up to 10 ft.   Flowers: Mid to late summer
Dense growth with grayish stems and bark. Leaves dark green above, lighter beneath, oval, pointed, serrate. Flowers very fragrant, small, white, in elongated terminal clusters. Fruit small dry capsules in fall, remaining over winter.
Habitat: Swamps, shorelines

Common Pipewort (*Eriocaulon septangulare*)
Wildflower   Height: up to 9 in.   Flowers: Summer to early fall
Aquatic or terrestrial plant. Leaves grasslike, translucent, in basal cluster. Flower whitish, tiny, in ½" wide knoblike cottony heads, emerges above water on 7-sided leafless stalk. Fruit thin-walled capsule.
Habitat: Bogs, shorelines

Pitcher Plant (*Sarracenia purpurea*)
Wildflower   Height: up to 1 ft   Flowers: Mid to late spring
Carnivorous. Leaves thick, hollow, pitcherlike, red or green, heavily veined, containing water. Insects, attracted by leaf secretions, are trapped in "pitcher" by downward-pointing hairs, are drowned and eventually absorbed as nutrients. Flower single, dark red, nodding, on long stalk. Fruit tiny seeds in pod.
Habitat: Bogs, swamps

Yellow Pond-lily (*Nuphar advena*)
Wildflower   Flowers: Late spring to late summer
Familiar floating aquatic plant with horizontal roots. Leaves leathery with waxy cuticle, up to 15" long and 9" wide, oval or heart-shaped, narrow notch at base, usually emergent. Flowers, on long stalk, yellow, spherical, 1"-3"; large outer sepals hide inner petals, surround inner disclike stigma. Fruit bottle-shaped capsule.
Habitat: Ponds, streams, shorelines

Floating-leaved Pondweed (*Potamogeton natans*)
Wildflower   Length: up to 4 ft.   Flowers: Mid to late summer
Rooted aquatic plant forming dense masses in quiet shallows. Submerged leaves long, swaying streamers; floating leaves thick, broad, oval, on long stems. Flowers pale green, tiny, clustered on emergent fingerlike spike. Fruit hard nutlet.
Habitat: Ponds, lakes, streams

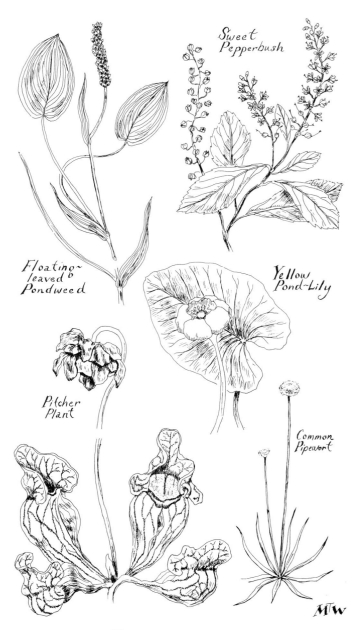

Sweet
Pepperbush

Floating-
leaved
Pondweed

Yellow
Pond-Lily

Pitcher
Plant

Common
Pipewort

MTW

Swamp Rose (*Rosa palustris*)
Shrub   Height: up to 8 ft.   Flowers: All summer
Very bushy; stems with short, down-curved thorns. Leaves compound, 5-9 leaflets, slender, ovoid, serrate; narrow stipules at leafstalk base. Flowers 2"-3", fragrant, pale pink or white, 5 petals, bristly calyx. Fruit achenes in fleshy, scarlet "hips" which often remain on plant all winter.
Habitat: Marshes, shorelines

Shadbush, Juneberry or Serviceberry (*Amelanchier arborea*)
Shrub   Height: up to 40 ft.   Flowers: Early to mid spring
Tall, often tree size, with light gray bark. Leaves grayish-green, oval, pointed, finely serrate, white fuzz beneath. Flowers before leaves, white, 5 narrow petals, long stalked in drooping clusters. Fruit like small apple, purplish, edible but dry; ripens in June.
Habitat: Swamps, shorelines

Mad-dog Skullcap (*Scutellaria lateriflora*)
Wildflower   Height: up to 3 ft.   Flowers: All summer
Erect or recumbent; thin square stems, branched; spreads by runners; smells minty when picked. Leaves opposite, ovate, pointed, serrate, smaller at top. Flowers small, bluish, tubular, lipped, on 1-sided raceme from leaf axils. Fruit nutlet.
Habitat: Marshes

Skunk Cabbage (*Symplocarpus foetidus*)
Wildflower   Height: up to 3 ft.   Flowers: Very early spring
Earliest spring bloomer. Leaves 1'-2' long, often 1' wide, basal, on long grooved stems, appearing after bloom. Flowers small, pale purple, on spadix in purplish/brownish or green, often mottled, spathe that resembles a bear claw. Fruit seed cluster. Plant smelly when crushed.
Habitat: Swamps, marshes

Swamp Smartweed (*Polygonum coccineum*)
Wildflower   Flowers: Mid to late summer
In groups, emergent or aquatic, indicative of changing water level (sometimes called "the botanical amphibian"). Leaves alternate, 6" long, narrow, elliptical, sheath swollen stem joints. Flowers tiny, pink or white, tightly clustered in terminal spike rising several inches above water. Fruit achene.
Habitat: Swamps, marshes, lakes, ponds, shorelines

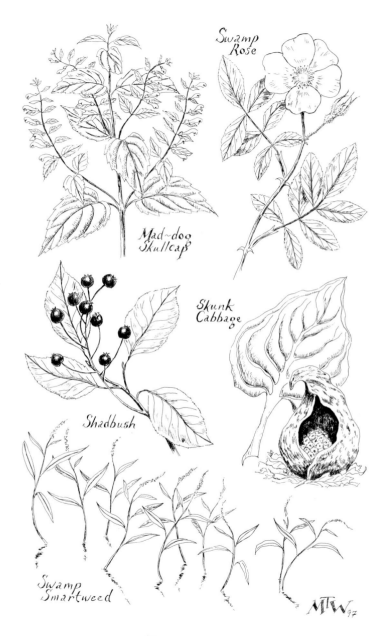

Swamp
Rose

Mad~dog
Skullcap

Skunk
Cabbage

Shadbush

Swamp
Smartweed

MTW97

35

Spicebush (*Lindera benzoin*)
Shrub   Height: up to 14 ft.   Flowers: Early to mid spring
"Forsythia of the woods", all parts very aromatic (spicy-scented) when crushed. Leaves 2"-5", alternate, dark green, smooth margins, elliptical. Flowers small, light yellow, clustered along branches, appearing before leaves. Fruit shiny, egg-shaped drupe, bright red, singly or in pairs.
Habitat: Swamps, shorelines

Marsh St. Johnswort (*Triadenum virginicum* = *Hypericum virginicum*)
Wildflower   Height: up to 2 ft.   Flowers: Mid to late summer
Slender wetlands perennial. Leaves opposite, 2", oval, pale green, pinkish veining, heart-shaped at base, clasping dark pink erect stalk. Flowers peduncled atop stalk and at leaf axils, pink, 5 sepals and petals, 3 groups of 3 prominent yellow stamens. Fruit oblong reddish capsule.
Habitat: Bogs, swamps, marshes

Water Starwort (*Callitriche palustris*)
Wildflower   Length: up to 10 in.   Flowers: Mid to late summer
Aquatic, mainly submerged, in cold or running water. Immersed leaves narrow, linear; floating leaves ovate, opposite, on weak, threadlike branching stems. Flowers tiny, green, in axils of floating leaves. Fruit oval, 1/10" long, flat, winged.
Habitat: Rivers, streams, lakes, ponds

Steeplebush (*Spiraea tomentosa*)
Shrub   Height: up to 5 ft.   Flowers: Summer to early fall
Low, sparsely-branched, woody light brown stems. Leaves alternate, 1"-3", elliptic, dark green above, whitish hairs beneath. Flowers pink or purple, tiny, densely clustered in terminal steeple-shaped spike. Fruit elongated seeds.
Habitat: Bogs, marshes

Poison Sumac (*Rhus vernix* = *Toxicodendron vernix*)
Shrub   Height: up to 20 ft.   Flowers: Late spring
DO NOT TOUCH! All parts highly toxic, cause severe skin rash. Only sumac in wetlands. Leaves alternate, large, compound, 7-13 leaflets 2"-4" long, ovate, pointed, smooth edged, short-stalked; shiny green, brilliant red in fall. Flowers greenish clusters from leaf axils. Fruit waxy, whitish berries in drooping clusters, usually persisting all winter. **Poison Ivy** (*Toxicodendron radicans* = *Rhus radicans*) (not illustrated) also very common in wetlands.
Habitat: Swamps, bogs, shorelines

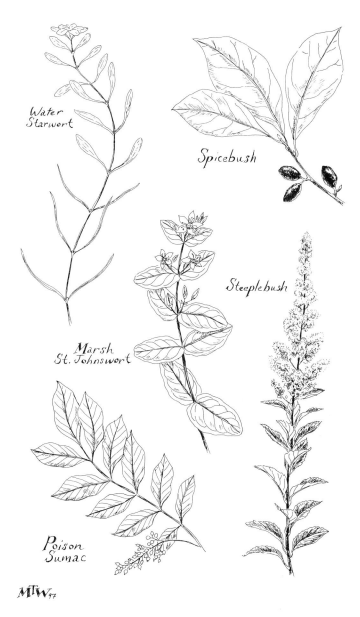

Water
Starwort

Spicebush

Steeplebush

Marsh
St. Johnswort

Poison
Sumac

MTW₉₇

Sundew
Wildflower   Height: variable   Flowers: Summer
Carnivorous; attract and entrap insects with sticky drops exuded by
reddish hairs on basal leaves. Enzymes reduce insects to nutrients for
absorption.
Habitat: Bogs

Round-leaved Sundew (*Drosera rotundifolia*)
Tiny, ground-hugging. Leaves circular, less than ½" on 1½"
leafstalks radiating outward. Flowers white, opening one at a
time, one-sided raceme on 4"-10" leafless stalk. Fruit pointed
seeds.

Spatulate-leaved Sundew (*Drosera intermedia*)
Similar to Round-leaved but leaves are longer and oval or spoon
shaped. Leafstalks more erect. Flowers white, on 2"-8" stalk.
Fruit oblong seeds.

Thread-leaved Sundew (*Drosera filiformis*)
More visible than other sundews. Leaves 6"-15" long, stringlike,
erect, quiver in slightest breeze. Flowers purple to reddish, one-
sided raceme on curved 8"-20" leafless stalk. Fruit spindle-
shaped seeds.

Swamp Sweetbells (*Leucothoe racemosa*)
Shrub   Height: up to 12 ft.   Flowers: Spring
Locally known as Fetterbush; deciduous; with upright branches,
reddish twigs. Leaves alternate, 1"-3", oblong, pointed, finely
serrate, short-petioled. Flowers fragrant, small, white, bell-shaped,
bracted, on one-sided raceme, usually blooming prior to leaves. Fruit
dry, 5-parted capsule in clusters, often remaining on stem in winter.
Habitat: Swamps, shorelines

Sweet Gale (*Myrica gale*)
Shrub   Height: up to 6 ft.   Flowers: Spring
Often found near Leatherleaf. Deciduous, dioecious; dark brown
twigs. Leaves alternate, 1"-3", wedge-shaped, serrate at tip, grayish-
green, resin dots beneath. Flower small ament before leaves. Fruit
nutlets in very distinctive cone-like catkins in summer. Spicy aroma.
Habitat: Swamps, marshes, bogs, shorelines

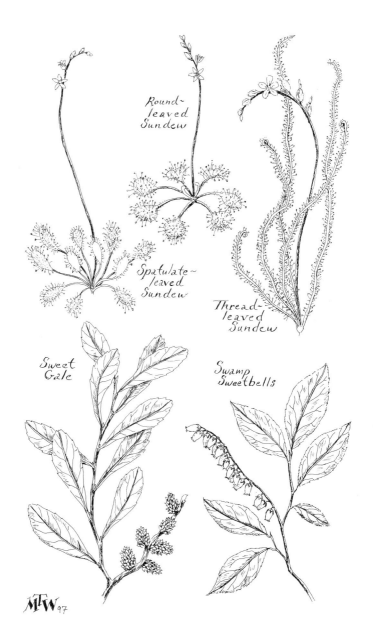

Round-
leaved
Sundew

Spatulate-
leaved
Sundew

Thread-
leaved
Sundew

Sweet
Gale

Swamp
Sweetbells

MTW 97

Turtlehead (*Chelone glabra*)
Wildflower   Height: up to 3 ft.   Flowers: Summer
Usually single plant or small clump, named for shape of blooms.
Leaves opposite, 3"-6", narrow, elliptic, serrate. Flowers in crowded
terminal cluster, white with pinkish tinge, tubular, upper lip arched
over lower. Fruit numerous winged seeds in ovoid capsule.
Habitat: Swamps, marshes, shorelines

Fragrant Water Lily (*Nymphaea odorata*)
Wildflower   Flowers: Summer
Very common, aquatic, with air-filled stems. Leaves floating, round,
4"-12", V-notched, shiny green, purplish beneath. Flowers, usually
open only in morning, white, floating, fragrant; tapering petals
diminish in size toward center, many yellow stamens. Fruit numerous seeds in fleshy submerged pod on coiled stalk.
Habitat: Ponds, slow streams

Water-milfoil (*Myriophyllum spicatum*)
Wildflower   Flowers: Summer
Submerged aquatic, in dense, weedy masses. Leaves numerous
(genus means "thousand leaves"), delicate-appearing, feathery, in
whorls of 4 or 5. Flowers tiny, purplish, on reddish emerged spike.
Fruit angled nutlets.
Habitat: Ponds, lakes, slow streams

Watercress (*Nasturtium officinale*)
Wildflower   Height: up to 4 in.   Flowers: Spring to mid fall
Naturalized from Europe. Low herb, floating on water or creeping on
mud; horizontal stems form thick masses. Leaves succulent, darkish
green, compound, 3-9 oval leaflets, terminal leaflet largest; pungent
tasting. Flowers small, white, 4 petals, in clusters. Fruit slender erect
seedpod.
Habitat: Streams, ponds, rivers

Pussy Willow (*Salix discolor*)
Shrub   Height: up to 20 ft.   Flowers: Late winter to early spring
Dioecious, multi-stemmed, rounded crown, stout branches; well-
known for furry buds.   Leaves alternate, elliptical, shiny green,
whitish beneath, stiff, serrate above middle. Flowers catkins, 2",
cylindrical, covered with soft, silky hair, before leaves. Fruit narrow
capsule, early spring.
Habitat: Swamps, shorelines

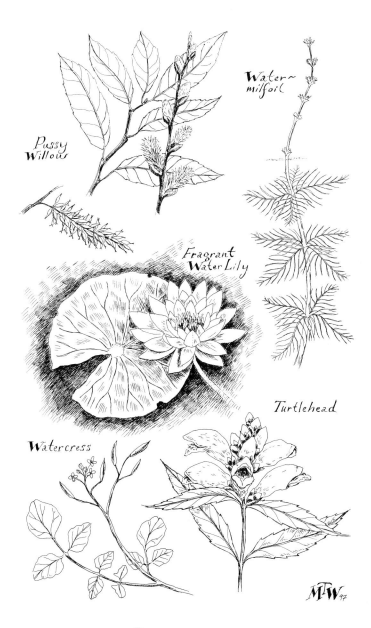

Pussy Willow

Water~milfoil

Fragrant Water Lily

Turtlehead

Watercress

MTW 97

SEDGES - Grasslike plants, with solid, usually triangular stems, "sedges have edges", closed leaf sheath.

Chair-makers' Rush or Three-Square Rush (*Scirpus americanus*)
Sedge   Height: up to 4 ft.   Flowers: Summer
Arise from long rootstock; acutely triangular stem, concave sides, tapering above flower.   Leaves 1-3, basal, elongate, shorter than stem. Flowers scaly reddish-brown spikelets out of stem's side. Fruit dark brown oblong achene in densely packed clusters.
Habitat: Marshes, swamps, shorelines

Spikerush (*Eleocharis* spp.)
Sedge   Height: up to 5 ft.   Flowers: Summer
Grow in clumps of matted rootstock; usually leafless with grasslike, slender, scaly green stems.   Flowers brown, minute, arranged in solitary terminal spikelets on stalks. Fruit tiny achene in clusters.
Habitat: Marshes, shorelines

GRASSES - Plants with round or flattened, jointed, hollow stems, split leaf sheath.

Common Reed (*Phragmites australis*)
Grass   Height: up to 15 ft.   Flowers: Late summer
Tallest non-woody plant in wetlands; abundant, invasive, forming dense stands.   Leaves blade-like, up to 20" long, 2" wide, smooth, stiff, sheaths loose and overlapping.   Flowers purplish plume-like panicle.   Fruit seeds in silky-bearded feathery terminal cluster. Spreads by long rhizomes and stolons. Indicative of disturbed natural environment.
Habitat: All wetlands

Rice Cut-grass (*Leersia oryzoides*)
Grass   Height: up to 4 ft.   Flowers: Late summer
Often in thick, entwined colonies; branched stalk thick, smooth. Leaves 3"-10" blades, pointed, scaly, sheaths short and rough. Flowers terminal panicle, up to 9", on drooping bloom stalks. Fruit oval seeds.
Habitat: Swamps, shorelines

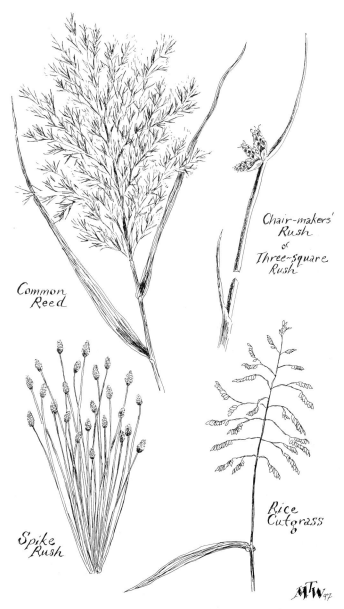

Common
Reed

Chair-makers'
Rush
or
Three-square
Rush

Spike
Rush

Rice
Cutgrass

MTW 97

43

FERNS - Seedless vascular plants. Generations alternate between inconspicuous heart-shaped gametophytes that produce sperm and eggs and larger sporophytes that propagate the species via wind-born spores; on Long Island, most are deciduous, some evergreen.

Cinnamon Fern (*Osmunda cinnamomea*)
Grows to 5 ft.; produces 2 types of fronds: green doubly-compound photosynthetic leaves, and brown, spike-shaped, spore-bearing fronds, which wither in late spring. Leaves emerge from rootstock in vase-shaped pattern.
Habitat: Swamps, marshes, shorelines

Marsh Fern (*Thelypteris palustris*)
Upright leaves up to 1.5 ft. Round sori produced on undersides of sub-leaflets. Stalk smooth, black near bottom, green near top. Leaflets nearly opposite each other along stem. Sub-leaflets often curl under. Found in extremely dense stands.
Habitat: Marshes, shorelines

Royal Fern (*Osmunda regalis*)
Doubly-compound leaves up to 6 ft., in clusters from rootstock. Large sterile sub-leaflets up to 1"; light brown fertile leaflets on top portion of some leaves. Usually found in standing water.
Habitat: Marshes, swamps, shorelines

Sensitive Fern (*Onoclea sensibilis*)
Up to 1 ft.; spreads rapidly by rhizomes. Photosynthetic leaves divided almost to stem, wavy margins on leaflets. Spore-bearing leaves have bead-like leaflets, green at first, turning brown and persisting through winter.
Habitat: Marshes, shorelines

Virginia Chain Fern (*Woodwardia virginica*)
Upright doubly-compound leaves up to 4 ft. on purplish stems. Leaves and leaflets widest in the middle. Sori in rows along center of sub-leaflets and axis of leaflets. Frequently occurs in standing water, often in full sun.
Habitat: Marshes, shorelines

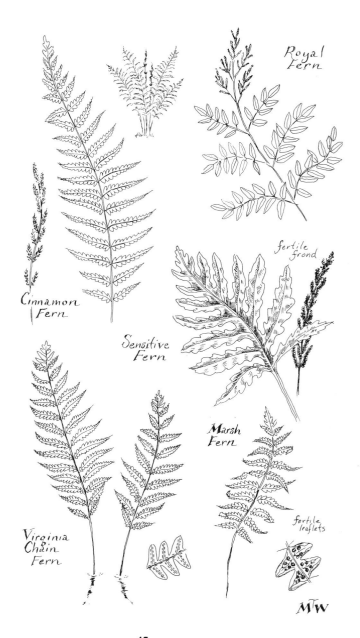

Royal Fern

Cinnamon Fern

fertile frond

Sensitive Fern

Marsh Fern

Virginia Chain Fern

fertile leaflets

MTW

HORSETAILS - Primitive relative of ferns with bamboolike stems from rhizomes. Alternate between sporophytes and male and female gametophytes.

Field Horsetail (*Equisetum arvense*)
Height: up to 2 ft.   Fertile stalk: Spring
Common, fast-spreading. Short-lived fertile stem resembles asparagus, tannish, leafless, dark sheaths, 1" terminal strobilus. Sterile stem green, multi-branched in whorls, sheathed. Prefers partial shade.
Habitat: Marshes, shorelines

BRYOPHYTES - Low-growing plants lacking woody tissues, true roots or leaves. Adhere to ground by rhizoids.

Three-lobed Bazzania (*Bazzania trilobata*)
Liverwort   Length: up to 5 in.
Small, prostrate, often forming dense mats on moist soil or rock crevices. "Leaves" dark green, 3 serrations on edge, tightly packed and overlapping in 2 rows along top of stem, 1 underneath.
Habitat: Swamps, marshes

Sphagnum Moss or Peat Moss (*Sphagnum* spp.)
Moss   Height: up to 1.5 in.
Dominant moss in wetlands. Evergreen; forms thick, spongy hummocks. Leaves pale or bright green, pointed, alive at top of stem, brown and dead at base. Empty cells allow absorption of water many times plant's weight. In bogs, dying matter accumulates into dense, floating rafts.
Habitat: Bogs, swamps, marshes

CLUBMOSSES - Vascular plants up to 6 in., alternating between subterranean gametophytes and larger sporophytes; stems prostrate on ground; spores in strobilus; small scale-like leaves.
Habitat: Bogs, marshes

Foxtail Clubmoss (*Lycopodium alopecuroides*)
Green, turning yellowish in winter; horizontal stems arching; strobilus bushy atop upright stem up to 1 ft.

Virginia (Bog) Clubmoss *(Lycopodium inundatum)*
Horizontal stems prostrate on ground, rooting as they grow. Vertical stems up to 8 in., bushy strobilus.

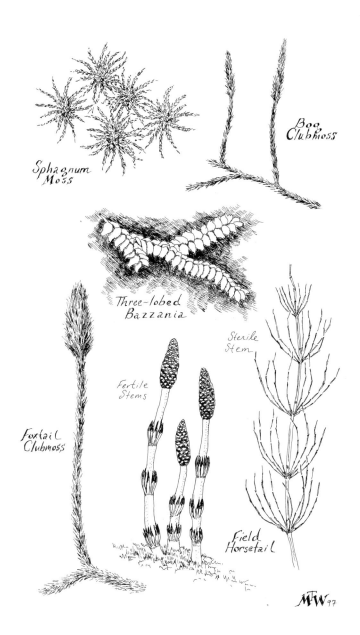

Sphagnum Moss

Bog Clubmoss

Three-lobed Bazzania

Sterile Stem

Fertile Stems

Foxtail Clubmoss

Field Horsetail

MTW 97

47

PARASITIC PLANTS - Lack leaves and chlorophyll, absorb nutrients from "host" plant.

Dodder (*Cuscuta gronovii*)
Vine   Flowers: Late summer
Usually found on shoreline plants, particularly Swamp Loosestrife. Resembles tangled yarn or spaghetti. Roots and base of parasite wither after yellowish-orange stem entwines around host.   Leaves alternate, minute scales. Flowers white, small, bell-like, in clusters. Fruit globose capsule with 1-4 seeds.
Habitat: Shorelines, marshes

FUNGI - Non-flowering, lack chlorophyll; consist of thallus (plant body) and mycelium (thread-like roots); parasitic or saphrophytic.

Sphagnum-bog Galerina (*Galerina tibicystis*)
Height: up to 8 in.   Appears: Late spring to fall
Tan mushroom, often abundant in sphagnum moss, especially during dry seasons.   Cap up to 1½" wide, conical, becoming somewhat knobbed, smooth; gills attached. Stalk hollow, long, thin.
Habitat: Bogs

Emetic Russula (*Russula emetica*)
Height: up to 4 in.   Appears: Late summer
Mildly poisonous mushroom; found singly or in groups, usually in sphagnum moss, rarely on rotting logs. Cap up to 3" wide, red to deep pink, cushion-shaped, becoming convex with depressed center, sticky; gills attached, yellowish-white. Stalk thick, club-shaped, wrinkled, whitish.
Habitat: Bogs

Fading Scarlet Waxy Cap (*Hygrophorus miniatus*)
Height: up to 2 in.   Appears: Summer to fall
Conspicuous small mushroom, seen among mosses, on rotting logs or on moist ground. Cap up to 2" wide, red, fading to orange or pale yellow, convex or flat, dry; gills attached, shiny, same color as cap. Stalk thin, smooth, scarlet, fading with age.
Habitat: Shorelines

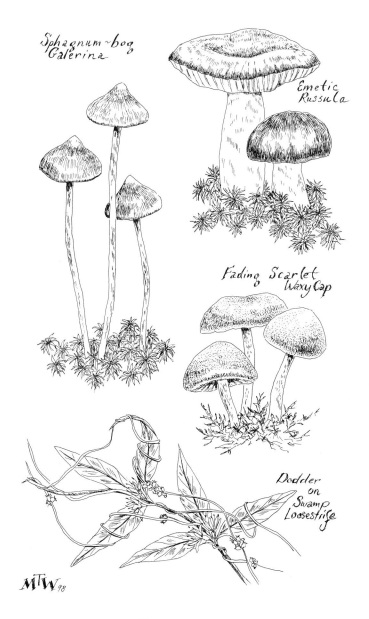

Sphagnum~bog
Galerina

Emetic
Russula

Fading Scarlet
Waxy Cap

Dodder
on
Swamp
Loosestrife

MTW 98

49

Animal Species

VERTEBRATES - Animals that have a backbone.

MAMMALS - Warm-blooded, with hair. Bear young live and nurse them with milk from mammary glands.

White-tailed Deer (*Odocoileus virginianus*)
Body height: up to 3.5 ft. at shoulder   Crepuscular
Ungulate; largest native animal on Long Island. Reddish-brown, graying in winter; white underside of raised tail used as warning flag. Antlers on male, 4 to 8 pointed, grown annually. Sleeps on ground, territorial. Herbivore, greens in summer, wood in winter. Fawns, 1 to 2, born late spring to early summer.
Habitat: Swamps, marshes, shorelines

Mink (*Mustela vison*)
Body length: up to 17 in.   Nocturnal
Weasel, always found near water, excellent swimmer. Thick dark brown fur, white patch on chin; small ears; slightly bushy tail. Sleeps in abandoned burrows and logs. Territorial carnivore, mainly frogs, fish, birds, small mammals. Bears 2 to 6 young in spring.
Habitat: Streams, rivers, lakes, ponds, marshes

Muskrat (*Ondatra zibethicus*)
Body length: up to 14 in.   Diurnal
Aquatic rodent, often seen swimming. Dense dark brown fur, paler beneath; long, scaly, hairless, rudderlike tail flattened vertically; slightly webbed hind feet. Sleeps in burrows or large conical houses constructed of vegetation. Omnivore, mainly aquatic plants, crayfish, clams. Bears 2 to 3 litters of 5-9 young during spring and summer.
Habitat: Swamps, marshes, ponds, lakes, rivers

Raccoon (*Procyon lotor*)
Body length: up to 28 in.   Nocturnal
"Garbage can bandit". Grizzled brownish-gray; pointed whitish face, black mask around eyes; black rings on 10" tail. Very vocal, somewhat sociable. Sleeps in tree hollow. Omnivore, consumes anything available, including fish, amphibians, and other aquatic animals. Bears 2 to 7, usually 4, young in spring.
Habitat: Shorelines, swamps, marshes

Mink

Muskrat

Raccoon

White-tailed
Deer

MTW 97

BIRDS - Warm-blooded, with feathers, two feet, wings, toothless beak.

Red-winged Blackbird (*Agelaius phoeniceus*)
Length: up to 9.5 in.   Migratory
Most common wetlands perching bird. Males black; distinctive red shoulder patch with yellow border on bottom; females and young brownish and heavily streaked. Song gurgling "kong-a-ree". Males arrive in late February to claim nesting sites. Omnivore, mainly seeds, some insects.
Habitat: Swamps, marshes, shorelines

American Coot (*Fulica americana*)
Length: up to 15 in.   Migratory
Ducklike aquatic bird. Grayish black, prominent white bill, white patch under tail; greenish legs, flanged feet, lobed toes. Call "kuk-kuk-kuk-kuk". Expert diver. Must patter on water for a distance to take off. Omnivore.
Habitat: Ponds, marshes

Canada Goose (*Branta canadensis*)
Length: up to 45 in.   Migratory and resident
Large waterfowl, seen at parks and golf courses or in V-shaped aerial formation. Brownish body, black head, neck, bill and feet; broad white chin strap, whitish belly. Call loud honking. Mates for life. Omnivore, mainly plants.
Habitat: Lakes, ponds, rivers, marshes, shorelines

Belted Kingfisher (*Ceryle alcyon*)
Length: up to 13 in.   Migratory
Pigeon-sized diving bird. Large, crested, blue-gray head; white collar and belly, blue-gray back and upper chest band (female with lower rusty band); large dagger-like bill. Call a loud rattle. Perches along waterways, then hovers and dives for food. Carnivore, mainly fish, crabs, lizards, mice, insects.
Habitat: Lakes, rivers, streams, marshes, ponds

Northern Harrier or Marsh Hawk (*Circus cyaneus*)
Length: up to 24 in.   Migratory, uncommon resident
Long-winged predator (48" span). Ovate ruff around face like owl, white rump, long tail. Male gray, white below; female and young brown, white with brown streaks below. Rarely vocal except "kee-kee-kee" at nest. Carnivore, hunts flying close to ground.
Habitat: Swamps, marshes

American
Coot

Belted
Kingfisher

Canada
Goose

Red~winged
Blackbird

Northern
Harrier

MW97

American Black Duck (*Anas rubripes*)
Length: up to 25 in.   Migratory
Dabbling or marsh duck. Very dark brown body, lighter yellowish-brown head, metallic purple speculum, prominent white wing linings, greenish bill. Female's call quack, male's croak. Springs from water at takeoff. Herbivore, dips over to feed at surface. Becoming less common on Long Island.
Habitat: Marshes, lakes, ponds, streams

Canvasback (*Aythya valisineria*)
Length: up to 24 in.   Migratory
Diving duck. Distinct sloping head and black bill; male whitish body, reddish head, black chest and tail; female gray-brown. Male's call croak, female's quack. Patters on water to take off. Omnivore, diving underwater for vegetation and small aquatic animals.
Habitat: Marshes, ponds, lakes

Mallard (*Anas platyrhynchos*)
Length: up to 27 in.   Migratory and resident
Extremely common dabbling or marsh duck. Male green head, white neck-ring, rusty breast, yellow bill; female mottled brown, orangish bill; both with bluish-purple speculum. Female's call loud quack, male's soft "kwek". Flies directly from water into air. Herbivore, surface feeding by dipping over.
Habitat: Ponds, lakes, marshes

Hooded Merganser (*Lophodytes cucullatus*)
Length: up to 19 in.   Migratory
Small diving duck. Male dark, blackish body, rusty sides, black-bordered white crest, slender toothed-edged bill; female gray-brown, darker head and crest. Call low grunt. Springs from water at takeoff. Carnivore, mainly fish, frogs, aquatic insects.
Habitat: Ponds, lakes, rivers

Wood Duck (*Aix sponsa*)
Length: up to 20 in.   Migratory
Small perching duck. Male very colorful, iridescent; white chin strap and throat; swept-back green crest, red bill and eyes, long square tail; female brownish, broad white eye ring. Call loud "woo-eek". Often perches in trees, springs into air at takeoff. Omnivore, both wetland and woodland plants, insects.
Habitat: Swamps, ponds, rivers, lakes, streams

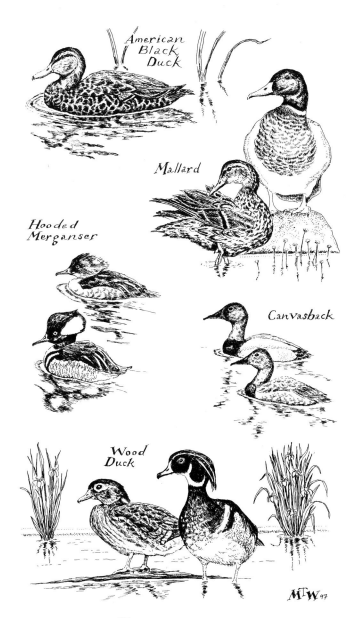

American
Black
Duck

Mallard

Hooded
Merganser

Canvasback

Wood
Duck

MTW 97

57

Heron family - Wading birds with daggerlike bills, legs trail in flight.

Great Egret (*Casmerodius albus*)
Length: up to 40 in. Migratory
Large heron; pure white body, black legs and feet, yellow bill. Breeding plumes extend beyond tail. Call deep hoarse croak. Hunts in shallows by stalking with neck outstretched. Carnivore, mainly fish, frogs, crustaceans.
Habitat: Marshes, ponds, streams

Snowy Egret (*Egretta thula*)
Length: up to 27 in. Migratory
Smallish heron; white body, black legs, golden yellow feet, black bill. Plumes on back long and lacy during breeding. Call low squawk. Hunts by shuffling feet and sprinting in shallows. Carnivore, mainly fish. Almost hunted to extinction for plumes, now protected.
Habitat: Marshes, ponds

Black-crowned Night Heron (*Nycticorax nycticorax*)
Length: up to 28 in. Migratory
Medium-sized, thickset, short-necked; black back and crest, white below, gray wings, pale legs, short black bill. White plumes from back of head during breeding. Call distinctive barking "guawk". Hunts at night moving briskly with lowered head. Carnivore, mainly fish, crustaceans, frogs, mollusks.
Habitat: Marshes, swamps, ponds, streams

Great Blue Heron (*Ardea herodias*)
Length: up to 52 in. Migratory, occasional resident
Largest heron, very common, with enormous wingspan. Bluish-gray body, whitish head and neck, black stripe over eyes, black legs, yellowish bill. Black plumes from crown during breeding. Call harsh "grahnk" when alarmed. Hunts in shallows, walking slowly or standing with head back on shoulders. Carnivore, mainly fish, frogs.
Habitat: Marshes, ponds, rivers, lakes

Green Heron (*Butorides striatus*)
Length: up to 22 in. Migratory
Small, dark green-gray body; chestnut head and chest, black crown, short yellow or orange legs, long dark green and yellow bill. Call sharp, piercing "skew" when alarmed. Hunts sitting with neck drawn in, then stabbing after few cautious steps. Carnivore, mainly fish, salamanders, insects, crayfish.
Habitat: Marshes, ponds, lakes, streams

Black-crowned
Night Heron

Great
Blue Heron

Great
Egret

Snowy
Egret

Green
Heron

MTW97

59

Osprey or Fish Hawk (*Pandion haliaetus*)
Length: up to 24 in.   Migratory
Predator, 70" wingspan, often seen nesting on elevated man-made platforms. Brownish-black above, white below (female's chest has dark marking), black line through eye and side of white head; conspicuous crook in wings when flying. Call whistled chirping. Hunts hovering over water, plunging feet-first. Carnivore, only fish.
Habitat: Marshes, lakes, rivers

Spotted Sandpiper (*Actitis macularia*)
Length: up to 7 in.   Migratory
Common shorebird. Olive-brown above, whitish below, large round spots on breast during breeding; white line over eye, white mark on shoulder, long sharp bill. Call distinctive "peet-weet". Constantly teeters up and down between steps. Carnivore, mainly insects, small crustaceans, marine worms.
Habitat: Ponds, lakes, streams, shorelines, rivers

Tree Swallow (*Iridoprocne bicolor*)
Length: up to 6 in.   Migratory
Perching bird. Body greenish metallic-blue above, clear white beneath; white cheeks, slightly forked tail, long, pointed wings. Song musical twitters. First swallow to arrive in spring, last to leave in fall. Omnivore, mainly winged insects over open water, seeds and berries in winter.
Habitat: Marshes, streams, lakes, ponds

Marsh Wren (*Cistothorus palustris*)
Length: up to 5 in.   Migratory
Small songbird. Body brown above, pale cream below, white eyebrow stripe, black and white streaks on back, slightly downcurved bill, cocked tail. Song reedy "cut-cut-trrrr", often at night. Female builds numerous football-shaped nests, most incomplete. Insectivore.
Habitat: Marshes, swamps

Common Yellowthroat (*Geothlypis trichas*)
Length: up to 5.5in.   Migratory
Wren-like warbler. Olive-brown above, bright yellow throat and breast, white belly; male has vivid black mask bordered above with white. Song familiar cheerful "witchity-witchity-witchity-witch". Most common small, yellow-throated bird in wetlands. Insectivore.
Habitat: Marshes, rivers, streams

Spotted
Sandpiper

Marsh
Wren

Osprey

Osprey
nest-platform

Tree
Swallow

Common
Yellowthroat

MTW97

REPTILES - Cold-blooded, with dry, scaly skin, sharp-claws (if legged); eggs in leathery covering. Hibernate.

Eastern Ribbon Snake (*Thamnophis sauritus*)
Length: up to 38 in.   Diurnal
Slim, semiaquatic garter snake. Yellow stripes along reddish-brown body (1 on back, 1 each side), belly light with dark stripes on margins, tail third of length, scales keeled. Always near water, swims at surface. Carnivore, mainly amphibians, fish, insects. Bears young live.
Habitat: Marshes, bogs, swamps, shorelines

Northern Water Snake (*Nerodia sipedon*)
Length: up to 55 in.   Diurnal and nocturnal
Aquatic. Highly variable in color and markings: from reddish, brown, gray to blackish; dark bands on neck, alternating dorsal and lateral blotches (more obvious on juveniles); double row of keeled scales under tail, belly spotted or plain. Swims both at surface and underwater. Carnivore, mainly frogs, fish.
Habitat: All wetlands

Eastern Mud Turtle (*Kinosternon subrubrum subrubrum*)
Shell length: up to 4 in.   Diurnal
Small, semiaquatic. Carapace olive-brown to black, no distinct markings; plastron yellowish, plain or mottled, 2 prominent hinges, pectoral scutes triangular; head spotted or streaked yellow, barbels on chin. Omnivore, mainly plants, some insects. Seen crawling along bottom in shallows, basking with just top of back exposed.
Habitat: Marshes, swamps, ponds

Painted Turtle (*Chrysemys picta*)
Shell length: up to 6 in.   Diurnal
Semiaquatic, commonly seen basking. Carapace olive to black, smooth, oval, flattened, plates bordered with olive, yellow or red; plastron plain yellow or spotted; yellow and red stripes on neck, legs and tail. Carnivore when young, herbivore at maturity. Prefers soft bottoms and half-submerged logs.
Habitat: Rivers, lakes, streams

Painted
Turtle

Eastern
Ribbon
Snake

Northern
Water
Snake

Eastern
Mud
Turtle

MTW 97

Red-eared Slider (*Trachemys scripta elegans*)
Shell length: up to 11 in.   Diurnal
Introduced, now widespread; semiaquatic. Carapace green in youth, almost black at maturity, oval; plastron yellow, often patterned; broad red stripe behind eye; lower jaw rounded. Carnivore when young, mainly herbivore later. Often seen on logs, basking stacked upon each other, diving quickly if disturbed. Crowding out native turtles, especially Painted Turtle.
Habitat: Swamps, ponds, lakes, streams, rivers

Snapping Turtle (*Chelydra serpentina*)
Shell length: up to 18 in.   Diurnal
Largest native turtle on Long Island; aquatic, aggressive. Carapace thick, rough, serrate, brown to black, 3 prominent keels lessen with age; small cross-shaped plastron; thick-scaled legs; large head, long saw-toothed tail. Omnivore, mainly invertebrates, fish, carrion, plants.
Habitat: Swamps, marshes, bogs, lakes, ponds, streams

Spotted Turtle (*Clemmys guttata*)
Shell length: up to 5 in.   Diurnal
Semiaquatic; seen mostly in spring. Carapace black, sprinkled with round yellow spots, no keel; plastron yellow with smudges; yellow and orange spots on head, legs and tail; male's eyes brown, female's yellow. Carnivore, usually insects, occasionally small animals. Commonly basks, enters water slowly if disturbed.
Habitat: Marshes, swamps, bogs, ponds, streams

AMPHIBIANS - Cold-blooded, usually moist-skinned; metamorphose from gill-breathing juvenile to air-breathing adult. Hibernate.

Red-spotted Newt (*Notophthalmus viridescens viridescens*)
Length: up to 5 in.   Nocturnal & diurnal
Aquatic salamander with terrestrial phase. Larva usually becomes **Red Eft:** red or orange land-dweller for 1-3 years, re-entering water as adult. Olive-green or brownish body with black dots, black-edged red spots on back, no costal grooves. Carnivore, insects, worms, tiny crustaceans, frogs' eggs. Toxin secreted by non-slimy skin protects from predators.
Habitat: Swamps, marshes, ponds, streams

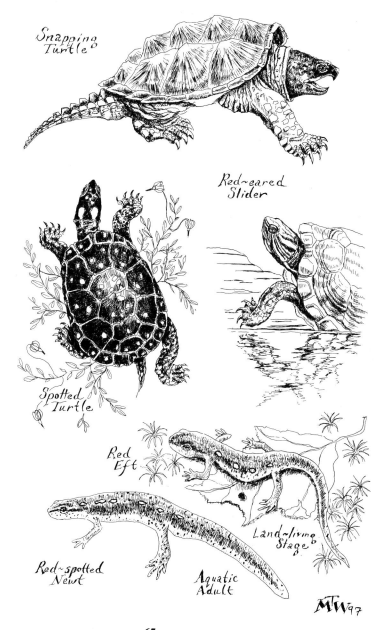

Snapping
Turtle

Red~eared
Slider

Spotted
Turtle

Red
Eft

Land~living
Stage

Red~spotted
Newt

Aquatic
Adult

MTW97

Spotted Salamander (*Ambystoma maculatum*)
Length: up to 10 in.   Nocturnal
Black to dark brown back, irregular rows of yellow or orange spots
from eye to tail, blackish belly, 11-13 costal grooves. Occasionally
found in wet soil under stones or boards. Carnivore, insects, worms.
Breeds early spring, eggs attached to submerged branches in ponds.
Habitat: Swamps, marshes, ponds, fishless streams (during breeding)

Eastern Tiger Salamander (*Ambystoma tigrinum tigrinum*)
Length: up to 13 in.   Nocturnal
World's largest terrestrial salamander. Dullish black; light olive or
yellowish spots, variable in shape and pattern, extend down sides,12-
13 costal grooves; belly olive, blotched; broad head, 1-2 tubercles on
soles of feet. Lives under moist debris. Voracious carnivore, worms,
insects, amphibians. Breeds very early spring, egg masses attached
to submerged materials.
Habitat: Ponds, lakes, streams (during breeding)

Fowler's Toad (*Bufo woodhousei fowleri*)
Size: up to 3 in.   Nocturnal
Very common. Brown or gray; dark warty blotches, pale line on back,
plain underneath; long parotoid gland touches cranial crest. Voice
trilling bleat. Found in moist areas with cover. Carnivore, mainly
insects, snails, worms. Breeds spring and summer, strings of eggs
laid in shallow water.
Habitat: Swamps, marshes, shorelines

Bullfrog (*Rana catesbeiana*)
Size: up to 8 in.   Nocturnal
Our largest frog, often seen at water's edge. Olive-green, dark
mottling on back and legs, yellowish mottled throat, pale belly; no
dorsolateral ridge; large tympanum on male. Voice distinctive deep,
resonating "jug-a-rum". Carnivore, insects, fish, frogs. Breeds late
spring, tadpoles mature in 2 years.
Habitat: Ponds, lakes, streams

Green Frog (*Rana clamitans*)
Size: up to 4 in.   Mostly nocturnal
Common in shallow water. Green to greenish-brown, dark blotches,
whitish underneath; dorsolateral ridges end before groin; yellow
throat and large tympanum on male. Voice twangy "banjo string",
single note or repeated. Carnivore, insects, small animals. Breeds
summer, 2-3 small egg masses.
Habitat: Swamps, ponds, lakes, streams

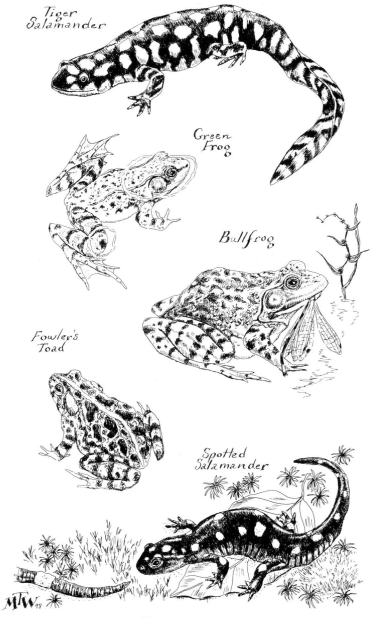

Tiger
Salamander

Green
Frog

Bullfrog

Fowler's
Toad

Spotted
Salamander

MTW '98

Spring Peeper (*Hyla crucifer*)
Size: up to 1.25 in.   Nocturnal
Treefrog. Smooth skin, brown, gray or olive, imperfect dark "x" on
back, whitish underneath; disk-like toe pads. Loud, shrill "peeping"
mating call at dusk is harbinger of spring. Insectivore. Egg mass laid
in water.
Habitat: Swamps, marshes, bogs

Pickerel Frog (*Rana palustris*)
Size: up to 3 in.   Nocturnal
Protected from predators by toxic skin secretion. Tan-skinned, dark
squarish spots in 2 parallel rows down back, dorsolateral ridges to
groin; whitish belly, undersides of hind legs yellow or orange. Voice
low croak or snore. Carnivore, mostly insects, worms. Breeds spring,
egg mass submerged.
Habitat: Swamps, bogs, streams

Gray Treefrog (*Hyla versicolor*)
Size: up to 2.5 in.   Nocturnal
Common. Warty skin, greenish, brownish, whitish or grayish, often
darker irregular markings on back; light spot under eye; inner thighs
orange and brown mottled, big toe pads. Able to change color in
response to environment and activity. Often well camouflaged on
tree bark. Voice strong, musical trill. Insectivore. Breeds spring, egg
mass laid in water.
Habitat: Swamps, marshes, shorelines

Wood Frog (*Rana sylvatica*)
Size: up to 3 in.   Diurnal
Often seen far from water. Variation in color pink to dark brown; dark
mask from eye, light line on upper jaw; prominent dorsolateral
ridges; white belly, often mottled. Voice raspy clacking quack.
Carnivore, insects, worms. Breeds very early spring, egg mass
submerged in icy waters.
Habitat: Swamps, marshes, shorelines

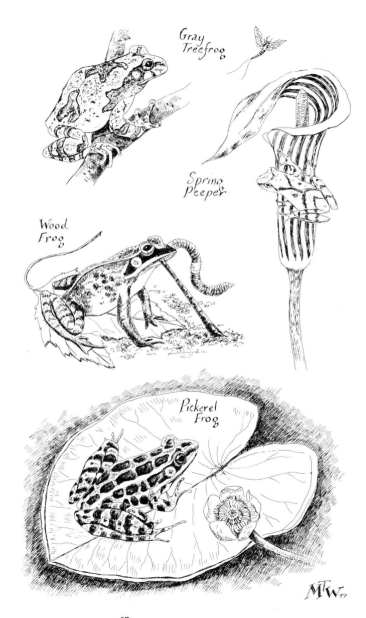

Gray
Treefrog

Spring
Peeper

Wood
Frog

Pickerel
Frog

MTW 97

69

FISH - Aquatic, cold-blooded, with fins and usually scales, breathe by means of gills.

Largemouth Bass (*Micropterus salmoides*)
Length: up to 38 in.   Introduced
Popular sport fish, common on Long Island. Elongate body, olive to brassy green, mottled, sides yellowish with black midlateral stripe; very large mouth extends beyond eye; spiny and soft dorsal fins nearly separate. Predator.
Habitat: Ponds, lakes, streams

Bluegill (*Lepomis macrochirus*)
Length: up to 12 in.   Introduced
Most common sunfish. Compressed body, olive back, yellowish sides, often dark vertical bars, blue sheen overall; whitish belly; long, pointed pectoral fin; large black splotch at rear of dorsal fin. Omnivore.
Habitat: Ponds, lakes, streams, rivers, swamps

Brown Bullhead (*Ictalurus nebulosus*)
Length: up to 18 in.   Native
Only Long Island catfish. Silvery to brown, dark mottling, whitish below; broad flat head, large mouth, dark barbels; sharp spines on dorsal and pectoral fins; lacks scales. Carnivore, bottom feeding at night in murky water.
Habitat: Rivers, lakes, streams

Common Carp (*Cyprinus carpio*)
Length: up to 36 in.   Introduced
Related to goldfish. Stout body, bronze to dark olive back, yellowish/silverish below; 2 barbels on each side of upper jaw; long dorsal fin with 1 serrate spine. Omnivore, rooting in mud. Introduced from Asia via Europe, considered threat to many native fish species.
Habitat: Rivers, streams, lakes, ponds

American Eel (*Anguilla rostrata*)
Length: up to 48 in.   Native
Long, snakelike; brownish or greenish above, yellowish white below; small head, lower jaw projects; dorsal fin far back and continuous with caudal and anal fins; tiny scales embedded in skin. Omnivore, including detritus. Catadromous, elvers developing in freshwater, migrating to ocean as adults.
Habitat: Rivers, streams

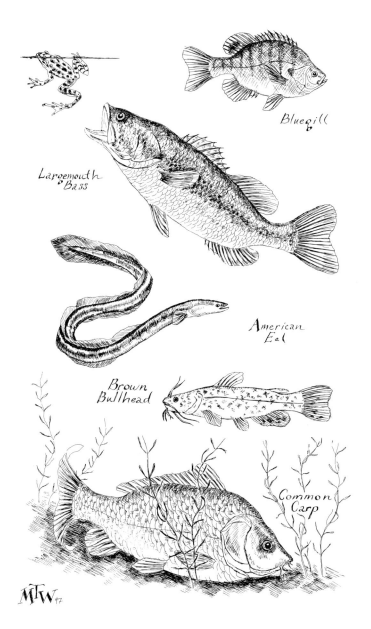

Bluegill

Largemouth
Bass

American
Eel

Brown
Bullhead

Common
Carp

MTW 97

71

Banded Killifish (*Fundulus diaphanus*)
Length: up to 5 in.   Native
Abundant on Long Island. Small, slender body, darkish olive to tan
with brown stripe on back, 15-20 dark bands on silvery sides,
yellowish below; flattened head, protruding lower jaw, small mouth;
squarish tail, dorsal fin far back. Insectivore, feeding at or near
surface in schools.
Habitat: Lakes, ponds, streams

Yellow Perch (*Perca flavescens*)
Length: up to 12 in.   Native
Oblong body, olive to bright yellow, 5-9 dark bars down sides; mouth
extends to middle of eye; 2 separate dorsal fins, first with black
blotch; forked tail. Carnivore, small fish, crustaceans. Crepuscular,
lives in schools in deep water, moving to shallows to feed.
Habitat: Ponds, lakes, streams

Chain Pickerel (*Esox niger*)
Length: up to 24 in.   Native
Popular sport fish. Cylindrical body, greenish-yellow above, distinctive dark chainlike markings on sides; belly whitish; very long
"ducklike" snout, dark bar under yellow eyes; 1 dorsal fin far back;
forked tail. Voracious predator, mainly fish, some frogs, mice.
Habitat: Lakes, ponds, swamps, streams, rivers

Pumpkinseed (*Lepomis gibbosus*)
Length: up to 10 in.   Native
Common sunfish. Compressed body, back greenish-gold mottled
orange, sides yellowish mottled orange and blue; belly yellow-
orange; small head, orange cheeks blue striped, black gill flap with
red or orange spot; long pointed pectoral fin, forked tail. Omnivore,
insects, crustaceans, plants.
Habitat: Ponds, lakes, streams, marshes

American Shad (*Alosa sapidissima*)
Length: up to 30 in.   Native
Compressed body, bluish or greenish above, silvery below; dark spot
with several small ones on shoulder behind gill; single dorsal fin;
forked tail; long anal fins; sawtooth-edged scales on belly. Omnivore, plant and animal matter. Anadromous, migrating in schools
from ocean to freshwater in spring.
Habitat: Rivers

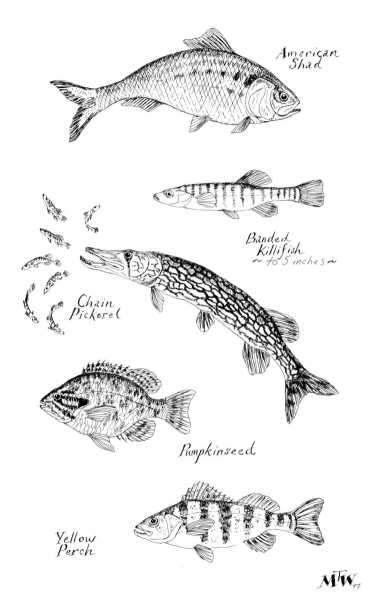

American
Shad

Banded
Killifish
~ to 5 inches ~

Chain
Pickerel

Pumpkinseed

Yellow
Perch

MTW 97

INVERTEBRATES - Animals that lack a backbone.

ARTHROPODS - "Joint-legged," segmented exoskeleton.

Backswimmer (Notonectidae)
Insecta - Order Hemiptera   Body length: up to .5 in.
Aquatic wedge-shaped bug. Back convex, keeled like a boat, usually pale gray or cream with dark markings; black underside; large eyes; short front legs grasp prey, long hair-fringed hind pair swim or "row". Carries bubble of air when submerged. Swims upside down. Predatory carnivore, insects, small fish.
Habitat: Ponds, lakes, streams

Predaceous Diving Beetle (Dytiscidae)
Insecta - Order Coleoptera   Body length: up to 1.5 in.
Oval, convex body, shiny brown-black, often with yellow markings; thin 11-segmented antennae; hind legs flattened, hair-fringed, for swimming. Traps air under wings hanging head down, tip of abdomen above water surface. Predatory carnivore, insects, tadpoles, newts, fish. Often attracted to lights at night.
Habitat: Streams, lakes, ponds

Whirligig Beetle (Gyrinidae)
Insecta - Order Coleoptera   Body length: up to .5 in.
"Streamlined", depressed, oval, shiny black with metallic sheen; short antennae enlarged, earlike; front legs long for grasping, middle and back legs short, flattened, for paddling. Eyes divided, simultaneously sees above and below water surface. Swims in jerky, gyrating motion, often in large colonies. Predatory carnivore and scavenger. If caught, may emit milky fluid with strong fruity odor.
Habitat: Ponds, streams, lakes

Water Boatman (Corixidae)
Insecta - Order Hemiptera   Body length: up to .5 in.
Similar to Backswimmer but swims upright in quick, darting manner. Oval, somewhat flattened, grayish or brown, fine markings on back. Front legs short, scoop-like for feeding; middle legs long, thin, clawed for holding; back legs fringed, paddle-like for rapid swimming. Rests horizontally under surface, often clinging to submerged vegetation. Carries bubbles of air under wings. Omnivore, algae, protozoa, debris.
Habitat: Ponds, lakes, streams

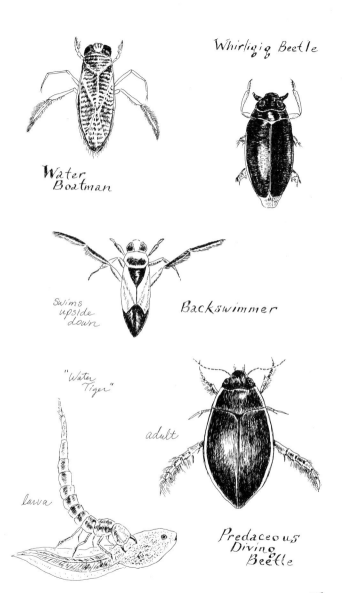

Whirligig Beetle

Water
Boatman

Swims
upside
down

Backswimmer

"Water
Tiger"

larva

adult

Predaceous
Diving
Beetle

MTW

Caddisfly
Insecta - Order Trichoptera   Body length: up to 1 in.
Terrestrial adult very short-lived. Slender, moth-like, usually brownish body; dull colored hairy, scaly wings held over back. Most of life spent as aquatic larvae, which usually build body-protective cases of silk, often covered with sand, leaves or other debris. Larva omnivore, adult drinks nectar.
Habitat: Streams, ponds, lakes

Black-winged Damselfly (*Calopteryx maculata*)
Insecta - Order Odonata   Body length: up to 1.9 in.
Frequently seen early to mid summer. Rather delicate, long, thin body; large compound eyes. Male shiny metallic green, wings black; female dullish dark brown, wings brownish, more transparent; white spot on front wing of each sex. Wings upward at rest. Aquatic nymph carnivore, adult insectivore.
Habitat: All wetlands

Green Darner (*Anax junius*)
Insecta - Order Odonata   Body length: up to 3 in.
One of fastest and largest dragonflies, 4½" wingspan. Black, yellow and blue spot in front of big compound eyes that touch on top of green head. Stout thorax green; long slender abdomen bluish, transparent wings iridescent. Wings held out at rest. Aquatic nymph voracious carnivore, adult insectivore.
Habitat: All wetlands

Mosquito (Culicidae)
Insecta - Order Diptera   Body length: up to .25 in.
Ubiquitous wetlands pest! Slender fly, small head, feathery antennae; narrow, clear, scaly wings; long, piercing mouth. Only female is "bloodsucker" for egg production; male drinks nectar. Aquatic larvae, called wrigglers, hatch from eggs laid on any still water.
Habitat: All wetlands

Water Strider or Pond Skaters (Gerridae)
Indecta - Order Hemiptera   Body length: up to .8 in.
Most commonly seen water bug; semiaquatic. Slender, flattened, blackish with gray velvety water-repellant hair; waterproof pads on feet; foreleg shortened for grasping; very long, thin mid and hind legs; wings usually absent. "Skates" on surface film, often in large numbers. Insectivore.
Habitat: Ponds, lakes, streams

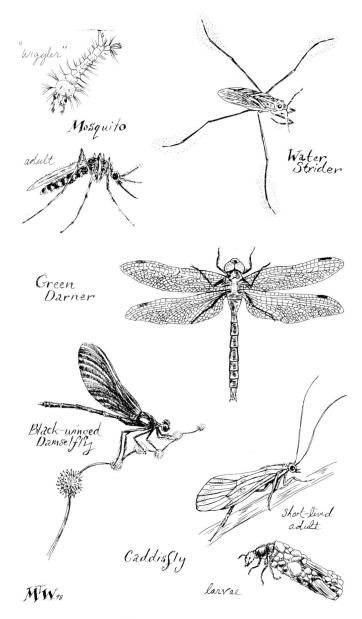

"Wiggler"

Mosquito

adult

Water Strider

Green Darner

Black-winged Damselfly

Caddisfly

Short-lived adult

larvae

MW 78

Spicebush Swallowtail (*Papilio troilus*)
Insecta - Order Lepidoptera   Wing span: up to 5 in.
Common butterfly. Forewings blackish, bordered with yellow spots; hindwings blackish at base, crescent shaped spots on border, bluish-green on rear half, orange spots at top and bottom. Larva eats Spicebush and Sassafras leaves, adult drinks nectar. Chrysalis overwinters.
Habitat: Shorelines, swamps, marshes

Six-spotted Fishing Spider (*Dolomedes triton*)
Arachnida - Order Araneae   Body length: up to .75 in.
Semiaquatic, with water-repellant hairs. Cephalothorax larger than abdomen in males; body dark greenish-brown, outlined with whitish stripe, 6 white spots down back; underside lighter color with 6 black spots between bases of very long legs. Walks on water surface or dives encased in air bubble. Carnivore.
Habitat: Ponds, streams, marshes, swamps

Crayfish (*Cambarus sp.*)
Crustacea - Order Decapoda   Body length: up to 5 in.
Related to and resembles lobster. Color variable to surroundings; carapace-covered cephalothorax, segmented abdomen with swim-merets; stalked eyes; 2 pairs of antennae; gills; 5 pairs of legs, first pair large claws; flat, jointed tail. Legs regenerate if lost. Nocturnal, hides in daylight. Omnivore.
Habitat: Streams, ponds, rivers, lakes

Amphipod (*Gammarus sp.*)
Crustacea - Order Amphipoda   Body length: up to .8 in.
Also called scuds or side-swimmers. Segmented body flattened sideways; no carapace; unstalked eyes; 2 pair antennae; gills; 7 pairs of thoracic walking legs, first 2 pairs for grasping; abdomen with "tail-limbs": 3 pairs of pleopods for swimming, 3 pairs of uropods for pushing. Nocturnal. Omnivore.
Habitat: Ponds, lakes, streams, rivers

FLATWORMS - Primitive; some free-living, most parasitic.

Planaria
Turbellaria - Order Tricladida   Body length: up to 1 in.
Common under rocks and debris. Very flat brown body, dorsal mottling; 2 eye spots between auricles; opening midway on pale underside functions as mouth and anus. Omnivore, mainly invertebrates.
Habitat: Lakes, ponds, marshes, streams

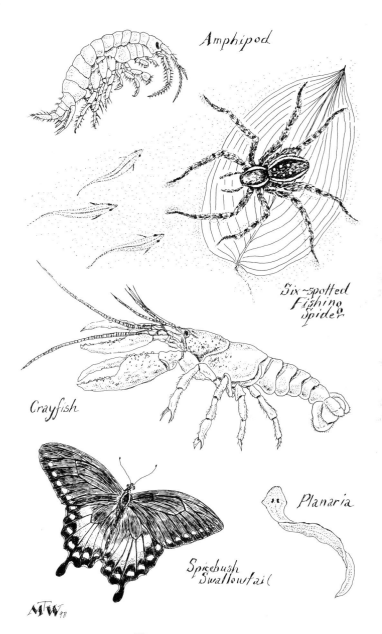

Amphipod

Six~spotted
Fishing
Spider

Crayfish

Planaria

Spicebush
Swallowtail

MTW₉₈

MOLLUSKS - Soft-bodied, usually with external shell.

Asiatic Clam (*Corbicula fluminea*)
Bivalvia - Order Veneroida   Size: up to 2.5 in. long, 2 in. high
Rapidly invading pest from southeast Asia; very common except on East End of Long Island. Shell triangular-shaped; exterior glossy, olive-green periostracum, umbone usually eroded, concentric raised ridges; hinge with sharp teeth; interior bluish-purple, shiny. Filter feeder.
Habitat: Rivers, ponds, lakes

Fragile Freshwater Mussel (*Pyganodon cataracta*)
Bivalvia - Order Unionoida   Size: up to 6 in. long, 3 in. high
Native. Found partially imbedded in muddy substrate. Shell elliptical, thin, inflated; exterior shiny, light to dark green; hinge lacking teeth; interior nacre iridescent, bluish. Filter feeder.
Habitat: Rivers, ponds, lakes

Three-whorled Ram's Horn (*Helisoma trivolvis*)
Gastropoda - Order Basommatopora   Size: up to 1 in. diameter
Pulmonate freshwater snail. Shell disk-shaped, yellowish to brown, sinistral, whorls with thick growth lines; spire depressed; lip expanded, thick; deep umbilicus. Herbivore.
Habitat: Rivers, ponds, lakes

Common Mystery Snail (*Viviparus georgianus*)
Gastropoda-Order Mesogastropod   Size: up to 1.5 in. high
Univalve originally from southern United States. Shell olive-green, shiny, frequently eroded, with 3-4 bands on the body whorl, rarely not banded; aperture less than half the shell size, lip black-lined. Chitinous operculum. Herbivore. Bears young live.
Habitat: Rivers, ponds, lakes

Three-whorled
Ram's Horn

Sideview

Asiatic
Clam

Common
Mystery
Snail

Fragile
Freshwater Mussel

M⊤W₉₈

GLOSSARY

Abdomen - Bottom or last section of arthropod body.

Achene - Small, hard, dry fruit with one seed.

Alternate - Leaves occurring on stem one after another, not opposite.

Ament - Long spike of unisexual flowers; catkin.

Anadromous - Migrating from ocean to breed in fresh water.

Annual - Plant that completes life cycle in one growing season.

Anther - Saclike part of flower stamen containing pollen.

Aperture - The opening of a shell.

Awns - Slender bristles or "beard" on head of grasses.

Auricles - Lateral projections from head of planaria.

Axil - Upper angle where leaf joins the stem.

Barbels - Small, fleshy, downward projections from mouth or chin.

Basal - Arising directly from roots; the bottom or base.

Bract - Modified leaf occurring below flower.

Calyx - Outer circle of floral leaves (sepals).

Carapace - Hard, bony, outer covering; shell.

Carnivore - Animal that eats only meat.

Catadromous - Migrating from fresh water to breed in ocean.

Catkin - Dense, elongated cluster of scalelike unisexual flowers.

Cephalothorax - United head and thorax.

Chitinous - Having horny substance which forms arthropod's exoskeleton.

Chlorophyll - Green pigment produced in leaves, essential to photosynthesis.

Chrysalis - Firm case enclosing insect pupa.

Cilia - Microscopic hairlike structures.

Compound - Composed of two or more similar but separate parts massed to common whole.

Costal grooves - Vertical grooves on sides of salamanders.

Crepuscular - Active at dusk and dawn.

Cyme - Flat flower cluster, central flowers unfolding first.

Detritus - Fragments of decaying plant or animal matter.

Dioecious - Having male and female flowers on separate plants.

Dorsal - Pertaining to the back.

Dorsolateral - Between center of the back and the side.

Drupe - Fleshy fruit with single seed in hard covering (pit).

Elvers - Young or baby eels.

Emergent - Plant rooted in water with most of vegetative growth above surface.

Enzymes - Biochemical catalysts in plant and animals.

Filter feeder - Animal that screens water flowing through body to obtain food.

Frond - Divided leaf of a fern.

Gill - Thin plate of tissue on underside of mushroom cap; organ in aquatic animals for extracting dissolved oxygen from water.

Globose - Spherical in shape.

Herbaceous - Referring to green plants lacking woody tissue that die at end of growing season.

Herbivore - Animal that eats only plants.

Hinge - Joint between two parts of bivalve mollusk.

Hummock - Low hill or mound of vegetation.

Insectivore - Animal that eats only insects.

Keel - Ridge down the back or along plastron of a turtle; ridge on snake scale.

Lanceolate - Lance-shaped, several times longer than wide, pointed at tip.

Larva - Immature stage of an insect, between egg and pupa.

Lateral - Of or on the side.

Metamorphosis - Distinct change in form undergone by an animal from embryo to adult stage.

Monoecious - Having stamens and pistils on the same plant.

Moraine - Unsorted rock and sediment deposited by a glacier.

Mycelium - Vegetative threadlike part of fungus, usually in substrate.

Nacre - Mother-of-pearl, internal layer of a mollusk shell.

Nutlet - Small, hard nut-like fruit.

Nymph - Immature insect that undergoes incomplete metamorphosis.

Omnivore - Animal that eats anything edible.

Operculum - Plate or "door" covering the opening in a snail shell.

Opposite - Arrangement of leaves directly across from each other on stem.

Ovate - Egg-shaped, with broadest part below middle.

Panicle - Loosely branched, pyramidal flower cluster.

Parotoid - External wartlike gland on toad's shoulder, neck or back of eye.

Peat - Partially decomposed plant matter, primarily sphagnum moss.

Pectoral - Of the chest; also paired fins attached to shoulder behind head of a fish.

Peduncle - Main stalk of a flower or flower cluster.

Perennial - Plant that lives three or more years.

Periostracum - Skinlike outer covering on many mollusk shells.

Petiole - Stalk of a leaf.

Photosynthetic - Able to use light to convert CO_2 and water to carbohydrates.

Pistil - Female organ of a flower, containing ovules.

Plastron - Lower shell on a turtle.

Pleopods - Brush-like limbs on abdomen of amphipod.

Pome - Fleshy fruit of the apple family.

Protozoa - A one-celled microorganism.

Pulmonate - Pertaining to the lungs.

Raceme - Elongated cluster of stalked flowers along a central stem.

Rhizome - Rootlike plant stem that forms shoots above and roots below.

Saprophytic - Flower producing but lacking chlorophyll and obtaining nutrients from decaying soil fungi.

Scutes - Enlarged shieldlike scales on a reptile.

Sepals - Leaflike structures surrounding the petals of a flower.

Serrate - Toothed on edge.

Sheathing - Tubular structure surrounding a part, as the lower portion of a leaf around the stem.

Sinistral - Left-handed or turning from right to left.

Sori - (singular - sorus) - Clusters of sporangia in ferns.

Spadix - Dense spike of tiny flowers, usually enclosed in a spathe.

Spathe - Leaflike bract, often large, enclosing the flower.

Speculum - Patch of distinctive color on wings of some ducks.

Spikelets - Small, elongated flower clusters.

Spire - Pointed tip of a snail shell.

Sporangia - Sacs in which spores are produced.

Stamen - Male reproductive organ of a flower.

Stigma - Top of female flower's pistil.

Stipule - Small leaflike appendage at bottom of leafstalk.

Stolon - Lower branch that roots.

Strobilus - Group of spore-bearing leaves forming a conelike structure.

Swimmerets - Modified legs on the abdomen of crustaceans.

Terminal cluster - Group which forms at the tip.

Thallus - Plant body not clearly differentiated into stem and leaf.

Thorax - Middle section of insect's body, bearing legs and wings.

Tubercle - Raised wart-like knob, often with spines.

Tympanum - Eardrum.

Umbilicus - Hollow at base of snail shell.

Umbo - Prominent part of bivalve above hinge.

Ungulate - Hoofed.

Uropods - Short, immobile rod-like limbs on tail of amphipod.

Utricle - Bladder-like organ; also one-seeded fruit with mature ovary.

Vascular - Forming vessels for circulation of fluids.

Whorl - Arrangement of leaves or petals radiating from a single axis.

ADDITIONAL SOURCES OF INFORMATION

Brockman, C. Frank. 1979. *Trees of North America* (Golden Field Guide Series). New York: Golden Press.

Caduto, Michael J. 1990. *Pond and Brook.* Hanover: University Press of New England.

Eastman, John. 1995. *Swamp and Bog*. Mechanicsburg, PA.; Stackpole Books.

Emerson, William K. and Jacobson, Morris K. 1976. *The American Museum of Natural History Guide to Shells.* New York: Alfred A. Knopf.

Geffen, Alice M. and Berglie, Carole. 1996. *Walks and Rambles on Long Island*. Woodstock, VT: Backcountry Publications.

Jorgensen, Neil. 1978. *A Sierra Club Naturalist's Guide to Southern New England.* San Francisco: Sierra Club Books.

Knobel, Edward. 1977. *Field Guide to the Grasses, Sedges and Rushes of the United States.* New York: Dover Publications, Inc.

Lincoff, Gary H. 1981. *National Audubon Society Field Guide to North American Mushrooms.* New York: Alfred A. Knopf.

Lyons, Janet and Jordan, Sandra. 1989. *Walking the Wetlands.* New York: John Wiley and Sons, Inc.

Muenscher, Walter Conrad. 1972. *Aquatic Plants of the United States.* Ithaca, NY: Comstock Publishing Co., Inc.

Nierina, William A. 1988. *Wetlands* (The Audubon Society Nature Guides). New York: Alfred A. Knopf.

Page, Lawrence M. and Burr, Brooks M. 1991 *A Field Guide to Freshwater Fishes* (The Peterson Field Guide Series). Boston: Houghton Mifflin Co.

Springer-Rushia, Linda and Stewart, Pamela G. 1996. *A Field Guide to Long Island's Woodlands.* Stony Brook, NY: Museum of L. I. Natural Sciences.

INDEX